The Spy who came in from the cold

Adapted by Michael Thomas from
The Spy who came in from the cold
by John le Carré

Hutchinson Educational

Hutchinson & Co (Publishers) Ltd
3 Fitzroy Square, London W1

London Melbourne Sydney Auckland
Wellington Johannesburg Cape Town
and agencies throughout the world

First published 1974
© Victor Gollancz Ltd 1963
© This adaptation Michael Thomas 1974

Set in Baskerville
Printed in Great Britain by
Anchor Press Ltd, Tiptree, Essex

ISBN 0 09 120131 4

1 Checkpoint

Leamas looked through the window of the checkpoint along the empty street.

'You cannot wait for ever,' said the American. 'Karl may come at some other time. Go and get some sleep.'

'No,' said Leamas. 'It's nearly dark now.'

Leamas was the director of the British spy ring in Germany. He was waiting for one of his men, Karl Riemeck, to escape from East Germany.

'But you cannot wait for ever,' said the American to Leamas. 'He is nine hours late.'

'If you want to go, go,' Leamas said. 'You have been very good. I will tell your boss that you have been damned good.'

'But how long will you wait?' said the American.

'Until he comes,' Leamas said. He walked over to the window and stood near the two policemen. They had their binoculars to their eyes. They were watching the checkpoint on the Eastern side.

'He is waiting for the dark,' Leamas said. 'I know he is.'

'This morning you said that he would come across with the workmen,' said the American.

Leamas got angry.

'Spies are not like aeroplanes,' he said. 'They do not have a timetable. He is on the run. He is frightened. Mundt is after him, now, at this very moment. He has only got one chance. He will choose his time.'

A bell rang inside the hut. They waited. A policeman said in German, 'Black Opel Rekord. One person in it.'

The American whispered:

'How did Mundt know about Karl?'

'Shut up,' said Leamas.

One of the policemen left the hut. He walked to the

1

sandbags just this side of the white line which marked the border. The other policeman waited until the first man was behind the sandbags. Then he took his black helmet and put it on. Suddenly the searchlights came on. The beams of light struck the road. It was like being in a theatre.

The policeman began his commentary.

'Car at first control. One person in it, a woman. Gone to East German hut for checks.'

Leamas waited silently.

'Checks over,' the policeman said. 'Gone to next control point.'

'Mr Leamas, is this your man?' the American said.

'Wait,' said Leamas.

'Where is the car now?' asked the American.

'Customs,' said Leamas.

Leamas watched the car. There were two East German sentries at the driver's door. One was talking to the driver. The other was waiting. Another sentry was walking round the car. He asked for the key. He went back to the boot, opened it and looked inside. Then he closed it and gave the key back to the driver. He walked up the road and joined another sentry. They stood together. The searchlights shone brightly on them.

The car drove up to them. They stopped it again, and again walked round it. Then they let it go across the line to the West. As it came closer Leamas saw that the driver was not Karl, but a woman. He knew her. Leamas pushed up the collar of his coat and said to the woman driver:

'Where is Karl?'

'They came for him,' she said. 'He ran for it. He took a bicycle.'

'Where did he go then?' asked Leamas.

'We had a room over a pub,' she said. 'He must have gone there. Then he will come across the border.'

'Will he come tonight?' asked Leamas.

'He said so,' the woman said. 'Mundt has caught all

the others.' Leamas looked at her. 'You say all of them have been caught,' he asked. 'Yes,' she said, 'they got the last one yesterday. If Karl is going to escape he has not got long.'

A policeman came up to Leamas. 'Move along,' he said. 'You must not stand about the border.'

Leamas turned round and said:

'Go to hell.'

The woman told Leamas to get into the car. 'We will drive to the corner,' she said.

Leamas got in.

Leamas took a key from his pocket.

'You will want somewhere to stay,' he said. 'Go to number 28A in the Durer-Strasse. I will phone you when Karl comes.'

'I will stay here with you,' she said.

'No,' said Leamas. 'Go to the flat. I will phone you.'

'But he is coming to this crossing point,' she said.

Leamas was surprised. 'Did he tell you that?' he said.

'Yes,' she said. 'He knows one of the sentries here. It may help. That is why he chose this crossing point.'

'And he told *you* that as well?' Leamas said.

'Yes,' she said. 'He trusts me. He tells me everything.'

'Hell,' Leamas said.

He gave her the key to the flat. Then he got out of the car and went back to the checkpoint. The policemen were whispering to each other when he went in. One of them turned his back on Leamas.

'I am sorry I shouted at you,' Leamas said. Then he opened his old case and searched in it. He brought out a half bottle of whisky. The policeman nodded and took it. He poured the whisky into three coffee mugs, then filled them up with black coffee.

'Where has the American gone?' Leamas said.

'Bed time,' said the policeman and they all laughed.

2 Escape

Leamas put down his mug and said:

'When can you shoot to help a man on the run from East Germany?'

'We can shoot only after he has crossed over the line,' said the older policeman.

'You mean he has got to have reached our side before you can fire?' asked Leamas.

'Yes,' said the policeman. 'We must not fire before he leaves the East German side. They say there would be a war if we did.'

'I've got a man coming over tonight,' said Leamas.

'Here? At this crossing point?' the policeman asked.

'It is very important that we get him out,' said Leamas. 'Mundt's men are looking for him.'

'Why doesn't he climb over the wall?' asked the younger policeman. 'There are still places where you can climb over.'

'He is not that kind of man. He will bluff his way through. He has got the right papers. He will be on a bicycle.'

They waited. Night came. Everything was quiet. The men spoke to one another very softly. There was only one light in the checkpoint hut. It was a small lamp with a green shade. But the big lights over the gate made the inside of the hut bright.

'Quick,' he said, 'There is a man coming. A man with a bicycle!'

Leamas went to the window. He picked up the binoculars.

It was Karl. Leamas knew him even at that distance. He was wearing an old mac and pushing his bicycle. 'He has made it,' thought Leamas. 'He *must* have made it.'

4

Karl had to go through two checks. They had looked at his papers and he was through the first check. Now he had to go through Customs. Leamas watched Karl lean his bicycle against the railings. He walked slowly to the Customs hut. He went in. He was in there for a long time. 'Don't be too long about it,' Leamas thought. At last Karl came out. He waved to the man at the barrier and the red and white pole swung slowly up. Karl began to ride towards the West German side. He had made it! He had only to get to the line, and past the East German sentry who stood on the line. Then he would be safe.

At that moment Karl seemed to hear some sound. He seemed to feel danger. He looked back, then began to ride as fast as he could go. The East German sentry on the line turned and watched Karl riding towards him.

Then all of a sudden, the searchlights came on. They were white and very bright. They fixed on Karl and held him in their beam. Then a siren began to sound. Orders were shouted.

In front of Leamas two West German policemen got down behind the sandbags. They got ready to use their rifles.

The East German sentry was still between Karl and the line. He took aim and fired as Karl rode towards him. Of course, he was firing away from the West German side into his own. So the West German police could not shoot to help Karl.

The first shot seemed to push Karl forward. The second seemed to pull him back. But he was still moving. He was still on his bicycle. He was passing the sentry, who was still firing at him. Then Karl fell to the ground. They heard the sound of the bicycle as it hit the road.

Leamas hoped to God that Karl was dead.

3 Return to London

Leamas was on the phone. He was on his way home to headquarters in London. He knew he was finished and there was nothing he could do about it. He had failed and he knew it. Mundt had beaten him. Until Mundt had joined the other side, Leamas had got good results. When Mundt had arrived, Leamas had known that it was all over.

Mundt was 42 years old. Leamas knew all about him. He knew his photograph. Mundt had blond hair and a hard face. He had found this out from spies who had deserted.

Until 1959 Mundt had worked as an East German spy in London. He had gone back to Germany very quickly after killing two of his own men to save himself. No one heard of him for over a year. Then he turned up at headquarters in East Germany. Soon he won a big struggle for power and became Director of Operations. Then one by one Leamas' spies were killed.

The first spy Leamas lost was a girl. She was not a very important spy. She used to do small jobs for Leamas. Mundt had her shot dead as she left a cinema. The police never found the killer. At first Leamas thought it must have been an accident. A month later a railway porter was found dead beside a railway track. Leamas knew that this was not an accident. Soon, another two of Leamas' spies were caught and put to death. That is how it went on. It frightened Leamas.

And now they had killed Karl, and Leamas was leaving Berlin. All his spies had been killed or captured. Mundt had won.

Leamas was a short man. His hair was grey and cut very short. He looked like a strong swimmer. His back, shoulders and neck were very strong. He had strong hands, with short fingers.

His clothes were ordinary. His shirts had button-down collars. He wore suede shoes with rubber soles.

His face was stubborn. He had small brown eyes. He looked like a man who could make trouble. He was mean with his money. He was not a gentleman.

The air hostess on the plane watched him closely. She said: 'If you want another whisky, you must hurry. We shall be in London airport in twenty minutes.'

'No more,' he said. He did not look at her. He was looking out of the window at the green fields of Kent.

Soon he would be back in London. He had failed.

4 At Headquarters

Fawley, a man from headquarters, met him at the airport and drove him to London.

'The Chief is pretty cross about Karl's death,' Fawley said.

'He was shot. Mundt got him,' Leamas said.

'Poor devil,' Fawley said.

'Exactly,' Leamas said.

Fawley did not like Leamas. Leamas did not care. He thought Fawley was a fool.

'What is the Chief going to do with me?' said Leamas.

'He will tell you himself,' Fawley said.

'Do you know?' Leamas said.

'Yes,' said Fawley.

'Then why the hell do you not tell me?' Leamas shouted.

'Sorry, old man,' Fawley said.

Leamas nearly lost his temper.

'Well, have I got to look for a flat in London?' Leamas said.

'I do not think so,' Fawley said.

They parked at a parking meter near headquarters. They went into the hall.

Leamas nodded to the doorman and got into the lift. The lift took him up to the Chief's floor. He knocked on the Chief's door.

The Chief opened the door. He shook Leamas' hand carefully.

'You must be very tired. Do sit down,' he said. His voice was just the same as Leamas remembered.

Leamas sat down in a chair facing a green electric fire with a bowl of water on top of it.

'Do you feel cold?' the Chief asked. He rubbed his hands together. He wore a black coat and a brown cardigan.

The Chief went to his desk and pressed a button. 'Would you like some coffee?' he asked. 'We will try to get some.'

He gave Leamas a cigarette.

Then Leamas said, 'Karl is dead.'

'Yes, indeed,' the Chief said. 'It is very bad luck. I suppose that woman gave him away.'

'I suppose so,' Leamas said. He did not ask how the Chief knew about the woman.

'Mundt had him shot,' the Chief said.

'Yes,' said Leamas.

The Chief stood up and walked around the room looking for an ash tray.

'How did you feel when Karl was shot?' the Chief asked. 'Did you see it? You did, didn't you?'

'I was annoyed,' Leamas said.

'But you must have been upset, too,' the Chief said.

'I was upset,' Leamas said.

'Did you like Karl?' the Chief asked.

'I suppose so,' said Leamas. He did not understand what the Chief was getting at.

'Karl was the last one,' the Chief said. 'If I remember

correctly the girl was the first to die. Then there was the railway porter, then the two men. It is just like the ten little niggers. Now Karl is gone.'

He grunted and said, 'I wonder if you have had enough?'

'What do you mean?' Leamas said.

'Are you tired of it all?'

There was a long silence. Then Leamas said, 'That is up to you.'

'You must not expect me to be sorry for you,' the Chief said. 'But you have had a hard time. Spying is a lonely job. It is like being out in the cold on your own. Do you understand me? Do you want to come in from the cold? Do you see what I mean?'

Leamas did understand. He remembered how lonely he had been.

'What do you want me to do?' he asked.

5 Operation Mundt

'I want you to stay out in the cold a bit longer,' the Chief said. 'Mundt must be killed. We must do this so that ordinary people can sleep safely in their beds. If we do not kill him, he will kill us. We must do the same as the enemy. That is why I think we must try to get rid of Mundt.'

'Why?' Leamas asked. 'We have lost everything in East Germany. Karl was the last. There is nothing now to save.'

The Chief sat down and looked at his hands. 'That is not quite true,' he said.

Leamas shrugged his shoulders. He could not understand what the Chief meant.

'Are you tired of spying?' the Chief asked. 'Please tell me if you are. If you are, we must find another way of dealing with Mundt. My plan is an unusual one.'

The girl brought in the coffee. She put the tray on the desk and poured out two cups. The Chief waited till she had left the room.

'What do you know about Mundt?' the Chief asked.

'He is a killer,' Leamas said. 'He was in London a few years ago. He had a spy working for him. He killed her.'

'Yes,' the Chief said. 'He tried to kill our friend George Smiley. He is a very unpleasant man. He was a member of the Hitler Youth. He enjoys the cold war.'

'Like us,' Leamas said.

The Chief did not see the joke.

'George Smiley knew a lot about Mundt. But he has left headquarters now. I think you should find him. He is writing a book about Germany – lives in Chelsea, in Bywater Street. Do you know it?'

'Yes,' Leamas said.

'Go and see Smiley,' the Chief said. 'He knows what I want to do. Then come and stay with me for the weekend. My wife is away, looking after her mother.'

'Thanks,' said Leamas. 'I would like to.'

'We can talk about Mundt in comfort then. I think you will make a lot of money out of this. You can keep all you make.'

'Thanks,' said Leamas.

'Are you *quite sure* you want to go through with this?' the Chief asked.

'If there is a chance to kill Mundt, I am ready,' said Leamas.

'I think you really mean that,' the Chief said. 'Please do not think that you *have* to say it. Are you sure you have got the nerve? They tell me that you walked about all night after Karl was shot. Is that right?'

'I went for a walk,' said Leamas.

'All night?' asked the Chief.

'Yes,' said Leamas.

'By the way,' the Chief said, 'if anyone asks how I have treated you, pretend I have treated you badly.'

6 Last Days at Headquarters

The Chief gave Leamas a small job at headquarters in the banking section. It was a simple job. He helped to send pay to spies in other countries. It was a job for men who had failed.

The people at headquarters were not surprised. They knew that Leamas had failed in Germany. They heard that the Chief had even stopped his pension.

Leamas suddenly changed. The change came very quickly. He started to drink heavily and became stupid. Even when he was sober, he did not understand simple things. He began to borrow money which he forgot to return. He was often late for work or left early. At first the others were sorry for him; they were afraid that the same thing might happen to them. But soon his bad manners and bad temper made them hate him. Soon no one spoke to him. Sometimes they pointed at him and said, 'That is Alec Leamas. He failed in Germany. How sad to see him looking like that!'

And then one day he disappeared. He did not say goodbye to anyone, not even the Chief. Some people said that he had stolen money. Others said they did not believe it. Leamas was too clever to do a thing like that.

For a week or two a few people wondered what had happened to him. But he had been so rude to everyone that no one was sorry he had gone. He passed out of the office and out of their lives.

Leamas went home. His flat was small and dirty, painted brown. From his window all he could see was the back of three stone warehouses. An Italian family lived over one of the warehouses. They had rows at night and beat carpets in the morning.

Leamas did not have much furniture. He bought

some shades to cover the light bulbs and two pairs of sheets for his bed. The rest he put up with. The curtains had flower patterns, the carpets were brown and worn out. The furniture was dark and ugly. He got hot water for a five pence piece from a yellow water heater.

People began to know Leamas. He had no friends and spoke to no one. They thought he was in trouble. He never knew the price of anything. The people in his street did not like him, but they were almost sorry for him. They thought he was dirty too. He did not shave at weekends and his shirts were dirty.

7 The Library

Every Thursday morning he went to the Labour Exchange and drew his money. Every time he went they told him he could have a job in the local library. He always said no. At last he took it.

'It is a big library,' the man at the Labour Exchange told him. 'They have thousands of books. They need another helper. The pay is good.'

Leamas thought that he had seen the man at the Labour Exchange before. But he took the job and went to find the library.

The library was like a church hall, and very cold. It had black oil stoves at each end and it smelled of paraffin. In the middle of the room sat the librarian, Miss Crail. Leamas was surprised that he was going to work for a woman. No one at the Labour Exchange had told him that.

He went up to her. 'I am the new helper,' he said. 'My name is Leamas.'

Miss Crail looked up from her work. 'Helper?' she said sharply. 'What do you mean, helper?'

'I have come from the Labour Exchange,' he said.

'You are Mr Leamas,' she said. 'You are from the

Labour Exchange. I see.'

At that moment the phone rang. Miss Crail picked it up and began to shout into it. Leamas left her to it and went towards the bookshelves. He saw a girl standing on a ladder. She was sorting big books.

'I am the new man,' Leamas said. 'My name is Leamas.'

She came down from the ladder and shook his hand.

'I am Liz Gold,' she said. 'Have you met Miss Crail?'

'Yes,' Leamas said, 'but she is on the phone at the moment.'

'What are you going to do?' Liz asked.

'I do not know,' he said.

Liz was a tall girl with long legs. She wore flat shoes to make her look shorter. Leamas thought she looked about twenty-two.

'Why not start work here?' said Liz. She pointed to the next section.

Leamas nodded. He went to the section and began to sort the books.

He sorted books until one o'clock. He felt very hungry and walked over to where Liz was sorting.

'What do you do for lunch?' he asked.

'I bring sandwiches,' she said. 'You can have some of mine if you like. There is no café for miles.'

Leamas shook his head.

'I will go out, thanks,' he said. 'I have some shopping to do.'

It was half past two when he came back. He smelt of whisky.

At six o'clock Liz said she was going home. They walked out together. Liz locked up and gave the keys to the porter. It was very cold outside.

'Got far to go?' said Leamas.

'Twenty minutes' walk. I always walk. Have you?' said Liz.

'Not very far,' Leamas said. 'Good night.'

He walked slowly back to his flat. He let himself in and pressed the light switch. Nothing happened. He tried the light in his kitchen and the electric fire by his bed. Still nothing happened. On the door mat was a letter. He picked it up and took it out on to the stairs. There was a bit more light there. The letter was from the electricity company. It said that he owed nine pounds, twenty-four pence. Until he paid he would have no electricity.

Leamas went on working in the library. He did his job quite well. But everything else he did got on Miss Crail's nerves. When she told him off he took no notice of her. She began to hate him, and stopped speaking to him.

8 Liz

About three weeks after Leamas began work at the library Liz asked him to supper. She asked him at five o'clock. She thought that he would not come if she asked him for the next day. Leamas did not seem keen to go, but in the end he did.

They walked to her flat through the rain. After this she asked him often. He came when she asked him. He never spoke much. Liz knew that there was something wrong with Leamas. She was afraid that one day he might disappear and she would never see him again. She tried to tell him this.

'You must go where you want to,' she said. 'I will never follow you, Alec.'

'I will tell you when I want to go,' Leamas said.

Her flat had only two rooms, a bed-sitting room and a kitchen. She had two armchairs, a bed and a bookcase full of paper-backs, which she never read.

After supper she talked and he lay on the bed, smoking. She never knew how much he heard. She did not care. She knelt by the bed holding his hand against her cheek, talking.

Then one evening she said to him.

'Alec, what do you believe in?'

Leamas shrugged his shoulders.

'But you must believe in something,' she said, 'something like God. I know you do. You have that strange look sometimes, as if you have something special to do. What is it, Alec? Do not smile.'

He shook his head.

'Sorry, Liz, you have got it wrong. I do not have any special beliefs and I do not like people who tell me how to think.'

She knew he was getting angry, but she could not stop herself.

'You have got some poison in your mind, Alec. You are like a man waiting to kill or something. I know you are, but I do not know what it is all about.'

His brown eyes turned towards her. When he spoke, Liz was frightened by the sound of his voice.

'If I were you,' he said, 'I would mind my own business.'

And then he smiled. He had not smiled like that before and Liz knew he was putting on the charm.

Later on they talked about it again. Leamas started it. He asked her if she believed in God.

'No, I do not believe in God,' Liz said. 'I believe in history.'

'Oh Liz,' he said. 'Oh no. You are not a Communist?'

She nodded and blushed.

She made him stay that night. They became lovers. He left at five o'clock in the morning.

He left her flat and went down the empty street towards the park. It was foggy. Twenty yards down the road was a man in a raincoat. As Leamas got near to the man the mist became thicker. Then it cleared and the man was gone.

9 Fever

Then one day about a week later he did not come to the library. Miss Crail was very happy. She went over and looked at his section to see if he had stolen anything. Liz kept out of her way for the rest of the day. She worked hard to keep her mind off Leamas. In the evening she walked home and cried herself to sleep.

The next morning she went to the library early. He did not come. As the morning went on she knew he would never come again. She had forgotten her sandwiches and so went out to get some lunch. She felt sick and empty, but not hungry. She had promised not to follow him. Should she go and find him?

She called a taxi and gave his address.

*

She went up his dark stairs and rang the bell on his door. She heard nothing. The bell seemed to be broken. There were three bottles of milk on the mat. She waited for a moment then she banged on the door. She heard a groan.

She rushed back down the stairs to the flat below and banged on the door. No reply.

So she ran down to the ground floor. She was in the back room of a grocer's shop. There was an old woman sitting in the corner of the room.

Liz shouted:

'The top flat. Somebody is very ill. Who has a key?'

The old woman looked at her for a moment, then called out, 'Arthur, come in here. There is a girl here.'

The grocer, in a brown overall and a grey hat, looked round the door.

'Girl?' he said.

'There is somebody very ill in the top flat,' Liz said.

'Have you got a key?'

'No,' said the grocer, 'but I have got a hammer.'

They rushed up the stairs.

The grocer knocked on the door and waited for an answer. He was out of breath. There was no answer.

'I did hear a groan,' Liz said. 'I know I did.'

'Will you pay for this door if I bust it?' said the grocer.

'Yes,' Liz said.

With three blows of the hammer he knocked out some of the door frame and the lock. Liz went in first. The man followed her in. It was very cold in the room and dark. On the bed in the corner lay a man.

'Oh God,' Liz thought, 'if he is dead I do not think I can touch him.'

She went to him. He was alive. She pulled the curtains back and knelt by his bed.

'I will call if I need you,' she said without looking behind her. The grocer nodded and went downstairs.

'Alec, what is it? What is making you ill?' she said softly.

Leamas moved his head on the pillow. His eyes were sunk deep in his face. His dark beard stood out against his pale cheeks.

'Alec, you must tell me, please, Alec,' she said. She was holding one of his hands in hers. Tears ran down her cheeks. She was at her wits' end. Then she got up and ran to the tiny kitchen. She put on the kettle. She did not know what she was going to make. Then she ran downstairs, into the street and into the chemist's shop. She bought some beef tea and a bottle of aspirin. The kettle was boiling when she got back to his flat.

She made beef tea like her mother used to. All the time she kept looking at him. She was afraid he might die.

At last he began to breathe more easily. The fever was going. Liz felt that the worst was over. Suddenly she saw that it was almost dark.

'Alec, please do not be cross,' she said. 'I will go. I promise I will, but let me make you a meal. You are ill. You cannot go on like this. You are . . . Oh Alec,' and she wept, holding both hands over her face. He let her cry, watching her with his brown eyes.

She came every day for six days. He did not speak to her much. Once she asked him if he loved her. He said that he did not believe in fairy tales.

On the Friday evening she found that he had dressed. He had not shaved. She wondered why. She felt frightened. Little things were missing from his room. His clock had gone and the cheap transistor radio that had been on the table. She wanted to ask him about this, but did not dare. She cooked eggs and ham for their supper. Leamas sat on the bed and smoked one cigarette after another. When supper was ready he went to the kitchen. He came back with a bottle of red wine.

He did not speak much at supper. Liz watched him. She became more afraid. At last she cried out:

'Alec . . . oh, Alec . . . what is it? Is it goodbye?'

He got up from the table, took her hands, and kissed her as he had never done before. He spoke softly to her. She was not really listening, because she knew it was the end. Nothing mattered any more.

'Goodbye, Liz,' he said. 'Goodbye.' Then he said, 'Do not follow me again. Not again.'

Liz nodded. She went out into the cold street. She was glad that it was dark. It hid her tears.

10 Prison

The next day was Saturday. In the morning Leamas went to the grocer's. He had no money. He ordered six things. The grocer wrapped them and put them into a carrier bag. They cost about a pound.

Leamas said, 'You must send me a bill for this.'

The grocer smiled. It was not a friendly smile.

'I am sorry,' he said. 'I cannot do that.'

Leamas noticed that the grocer did not say 'Sir.'

'Why the hell not?' Leamas asked.

'I do not know you,' said the grocer.

'Don't be silly,' said Leamas. 'I have done my shopping here for months.' The grocer blushed.

'Can I see your banker's card?' he said.

'Don't talk nonsense,' Leamas said. 'The people who shop here never go inside a bank.'

The people in the queue knew this was true.

'I do not know you,' the grocer said again. 'And I do not like you. Now get out of my shop.'

Leamas was holding the carrier bag. The grocer grabbed it. The other people watched. Some said the grocer pushed Leamas. Others said he did not. Anyhow Leamas hit him twice, without letting go of the carrier bag.

He seemed to hit him with the side of his left hand and with his left elbow at the same time.

The grocer fell and lay like a rock. The grocer's cheek bone and jaw were broken. The newspapers reported it without much fuss.

In court Leamas pleaded guilty. He was sent to prison for three months.

Every night he lay on his bed in his cell. He listened to the other prisoners. There was a boy who sobbed. There was also an old prisoner who sang all the time, using his food tin as a drum. There was an Irishman. He sang songs about the IRA.

They gave him a brown paper parcel when he left prison. In it were all his belongings. The prison governor asked him what he was going to do. Leamas said that he would try to make a fresh start. The governor said that that was a good idea.

The probation officer asked Leamas if he would like to be a male nurse. Leamas said he would try it. The job was in Buckinghamshire. He took the address and the times of the trains.

So he left prison.

He took a bus to Marble Arch. Then he walked. He had a bit of money in his pocket, so he went for a meal.

He walked through Hyde Park to Piccadilly. Then he went through Green Park and St James's Park to Parliament Square. Then he went down Whitehall to the Strand.

He went into the big café near Charing Cross Station. He bought a steak for sixty pence.

London was beautiful that day. The parks were full of crocuses and daffodils. The wind was blowing and he could have walked all day. But he still had his brown paper parcel. He had to get rid of it. How could he? The litter baskets were too small. He sat down on a seat and put the parcel beside him. Then he moved along the seat a little way. After a few minutes he got up and walked away, leaving the parcel. He had just reached the path when he heard a shout. He turned. He saw a man in an army mac calling him. He was holding up the brown paper parcel.

Leamas took no notice of him. He just walked on along the path. He heard the man shout again. He took no notice. He heard footsteps close behind him. Then he heard a voice. It said:

'Here, you – I say!'

'Yes?' said Leamas.

'This is your parcel, is it not?' the man said. 'You left it on the seat. Why did you not stop when I called?'

Leamas looked at the man. He was tall, with curly brown hair. He wore an orange tie and a pale green shirt. Leamas thought he might be a schoolmaster. His eyes looked weak.

'You can put it back,' said Leamas. 'I do not want it.'

The man blushed.

'You can't just leave it there,' he said. 'It is litter.'

'I can,' said Leamas. 'Somebody will find a use for it.'

Leamas tried to move on, but the man stood in front of him. He held out the parcel in both arms, like a baby. 'Get out of my way,' Leamas said. 'Do you mind?'

'Look here,' said the man. 'I was trying to do you a favour. Why are you so damned rude?'

'If you are doing me a favour,' Leamas said, 'Why have you been following me for the last half hour?'

The man did not move. He must have been shaken by what Leamas said. But he did not show it.

He said, 'I thought you were somebody I knew in Berlin. I saw you in Marble Arch. I thought you were Alec Leamas. I borrowed money from Alec Leamas in Berlin. I used to be in the BBC. I followed you to make sure that you were Leamas.'

Leamas went on looking at him. At last he said:

'I am Leamas. Who the hell are you?'

11 Contact

He said his name was Ashe. 'Ashe with an "E"', he said. Leamas knew that he was lying. Ashe pretended that he was not sure that Leamas was Leamas. Then he ordered lunch. He did not seem to mind how much it cost. This made Leamas suspicious. They drank some German wine to remind them of the good old days. Leamas said that he could not remember Ashe. Ashe said that he was surprised.

Ashe was a soft man. Leamas saw this. It made Leamas want to bully him. Leamas was rude to Ashe for over an hour. Ashe took it all. Leamas thought that Ashe must be up to no good. Otherwise he would not have put up with Leamas' rudeness.

It was nearly four o'clock when they asked for their bill. Ashe paid. Then he took out his cheque book to pay Leamas back what he owed.

'I say,' Ashe said, 'a cheque is all right, is it?'

Leamas blushed and said,

'Not really. I have no bank at the moment. I have only just come back from abroad. I have not fixed up a bank yet. I will cash the cheque at your bank.'

'My dear chap,' Ashe said, 'You must not do that. You would have to go to the other side of London.'

Leamas shrugged his shoulders. Ashe laughed and said that he would bring the money in cash on the next day. He would come to the same place at one o'clock.

*

Ashe got into a taxi. Leamas waved until it was out of sight. When it was gone, he looked at his watch. It was four o'clock. He felt that he was still being followed. And so he walked down to Fleet Street.

He had a cup of coffee in the Black and White. He looked at bookshops and read the evening papers in the windows of the newspaper offices. He jumped on a bus. The bus went to Ludgate Hill. It was held up in a traffic jam near a tube station. He got off and caught a tube. He bought a 5p ticket. He stood in the end carriage and got off at the next station. He got on another train to Euston.

Then he walked back to Charing Cross.

It was nine o'clock when he reached the station. It was cold. There was a van waiting outside the station. The driver was fast asleep. Leamas looked at the number. He went over and called through the window:

'Are you from Clements?' Leamas said.

The driver woke up and said:

'Mr Thomas?'

'No,' said Leamas. 'Thomas could not come. I am Amies from Hounslow.'

'Jump in, Mr Amies,' the driver said, and opened the door. They drove towards Chelsea. The driver knew the way.

The van stopped in Bywater Street. Leamas got out

and knocked at a door.

The Chief opened the door.

'Come in,' the Chief said. 'George Smiley is out. I have borrowed his house.' Not until Leamas was inside and the front door was shut, did the Chief put on the light.

'They picked me up this morning,' Leamas said. 'A man called Ashe. We are meeting again tomorrow.'

Leamas told his story to the Chief. He told him everything about hitting the grocer, about prison, about meeting Ashe that morning. The Chief listened carefully.

'How did you like prison?' the Chief said. 'I am sorry that we could not make it more comfortable for you.'

'Of course you could not,' said Leamas.

'We have to be careful, you know,' said the Chief. 'I hear you were ill. I am sorry. What was the matter?'

'Just fever,' Leamas said.

'How long were you in bed?' asked the Chief.

'About ten days,' said Leamas.

'How awful. And nobody to look after you, of course,' the Chief said.

Leamas said nothing for a long time.

'You know that Liz is a Communist, don't you?' said the Chief quietly.

'Yes,' said Leamas. 'I do not want her brought into this.'

'Why should she be?' said the Chief. 'Who said that she would be?'

'No one,' said Leamas. 'I just want to make sure. I know what happens in spy business. I do not want her to be brought into it.'

'Oh, quite, quite,' the Chief said.

'And who is that man in the Labour Exchange?' asked Leamas. 'I think he worked in headquarters in the war. I think his name is Pitt.'

'I do not know anyone in the Labour Exchange,' said

the Chief. 'Did you say his name was Pitt?'

'Yes,' said Leamas.

'No,' said the Chief, 'a new name to me. In the Labour Exchange did you say?'

'Oh! for God's sake,' said Leamas.

'I am sorry,' said the Chief, 'I am forgetting my duty. Would you like a drink?'

'No,' said Leamas. 'I want to go away tonight. I want to go to the country. Is the house open?'

'Yes,' said the Chief. 'I have a car ready for you. You must see a doctor about your fever.'

'I do not need a doctor,' said Leamas.

'Do what you like,' said the Chief.

'Why is Smiley not here?' asked Leamas.

'He does not like the plan,' said the Chief. 'He knows it must be done. But he does not want to join in. He told you about Mundt, though, didn't he?'

'Yes,' said Leamas.

'Mundt is a very hard man,' the Chief said. 'We must never forget that. And he is a very good spy.'

'Does Smiley know why we are after Mundt?' Leamas said.

The Chief nodded.

'And he still does not like it?' said Leamas.

'No,' said the Chief. 'He does not think it is right to kill. He wants others to do it.'

'Tell me,' Leamas said, 'how are you sure that killing Mundt will give us what we want?'

'Do not worry,' the Chief said. 'All that has been taken care of.'

They walked to the door. The Chief put his hand on Leamas' shoulder.

'This is your last job,' he said. 'Then you can come in from the cold.'

Then the Chief added:

'Do you want me to do anything about that girl? Money, or anything?'

'No,' said Leamas. 'I will look after her when it is all

over. I just want you to leave her alone. I want you to forget her.'

He nodded to the Chief and went out into the night. Into the cold.

12 Ashe and Kiever

The next day Leamas went to meet Ashe. He got there twenty minutes late and smelt of whisky. Ashe seemed very glad to see him. He said that he had only just come. He gave Leamas an envelope with ten pounds in it.

'All in pound notes,' he said. 'I hope that's all right?'

'Thanks,' Leamas said. 'Let's have a drink.' He had not shaved and his collar was filthy. He called the waiter and ordered a large whisky for himself and a pink gin for Ashe. Leamas' hand shook when he poured the soda water into his glass. He almost slopped it over the side.

They had a good lunch, with a lot to drink. Ashe did most of the talking. He started by talking about himself. Leamas had expected this.

'I've got on to a good thing,' he said. 'I write reports in English for foreign newspapers. When I left Berlin I made a mess of things. I started a weekly newspaper about hobbies for the over-sixties. . . . A dreadful paper! A printing strike finished it. One day I got a letter from an old friend, Sam Kiever. He worked for some foreign newspapers. He asked me to write about English life for him. You know the sort of thing – six hundred words on Morris dancing! Kiever translated it and sent it off.'

Ashe stopped talking. He waited for Leamas to say something about himself. Leamas said nothing.

Ashe said, 'Shall I order some wine?'

Leamas said he would stick to whisky. By the time

the coffee came he had drunk four large ones. He was in a bad way.

Ashe was silent for a moment.

Then he said, 'You don't know Sam, do you?'

'Sam?' said Leamas. 'Which Sam?'

Ashe was annoyed.

'Sam Kiever,' he said, 'my boss. The chap I have been telling you about.'

'Was he in Berlin too?' Leamas said.

'No,' said Ashe, 'but he knows Germany. He worked in Bonn once, but not in Berlin. Do you know him? He's a dear.'

'Don't think so,' said Leamas.

There was another silence. Then Ashe said, 'What do you do these days, old chap?'

'I'm on the shelf,' Leamas said. He grinned a bit stupidly.

'I forget what you were doing in Berlin,' Ashe said. 'Weren't you mixed up in the Cold War?'

Now he is getting to the point, Leamas said to himself.

Leamas blushed and then said, 'I was an office boy for the Yanks, like the rest of us.'

'You must meet Sam,' Ashe said. 'You will like him. Where can I find you?'

'You can't,' said Leamas in a tired voice.

'I don't understand, old chap,' said Ashe. 'Where are you staying?'

'I don't live anywhere,' said Leamas. 'I haven't got a job. And they are too mean to give me a pension.'

Ashe said, 'But that's awful. Why didn't you tell me? Why not come and stay at my place? It's only small, but there is room for one more if you don't mind a camp bed. You can't just live in the trees, my dear chap!'

'I'm all right for a bit,' said Leamas. He tapped the pocket with the money in it. 'I'm going to get a job. I'll get one in a week or so. Then I'll be all right.'

'What sort of job?' Ashe said.

'Oh, I don't know,' Leamas said. 'Anything.'

'But you can't take just *anything*, Alec,' Ashe said. 'You speak German like a native. There must be all sorts of things you can do.'

'I've done all sorts of things,' Leamas said. 'I've sold books from door to door. I've sorted books in a library. I've worked in a stinking glue factory. What the hell *can* I do?'

'But, Alec,' he said, 'you need contacts. I know what it is like. I've been out of work myself. This is when you must *know* people. If I had not met Sam five years ago I would still be out of work. Look, Alec, come and stay with me for a week. We will ask Sam round and some of his newspaper friends from Berlin.'

'But I can't write,' said Leamas. 'I couldn't write a damn thing.'

Ashe put his hand on Leamas' arm. 'Now, don't fuss,' he said. 'Let's take things one at a time. Where are your bits and pieces?'

'My what?' said Leamas.

'Your things,' Ashe said. 'Your clothes and bag.'

'I haven't got any,' Leamas said. 'I've sold all I had – except the parcel.'

'What parcel?' Ashe said.

'The brown paper parcel you picked up in the park,' Leamas said. 'The one I was trying to throw away.'

They went to Ashe's flat in Dolphin Square. It was just as Leamas had thought. It was small and ordinary. Ashe had some things from Germany, some beer mugs and a pipe.

Ashe made tea and they drank it. Leamas did not say a word. Even Ashe was quiet.

After tea Ashe said, 'I'm going out to do a bit of shopping before the shops close. Then we will decide what to do. I'll phone Sam later on. You two must get together. Why don't you get some sleep – you look all in.'

Leamas nodded. 'It's damn good of you,' he said.

Ashe patted him on the shoulder. Then he picked up his army mac and went out.

As soon as Leamas thought that Ashe was out of the building, he got up. He left the front door of the flat on the latch. Then he went downstairs to the hall. There were two phone boxes. He phoned a Maida Vale number and asked for Mr Thomas's secretary. A girl's voice said, 'Mr Thomas's secretary speaking.'

'I am phoning for Mr Sam Kiever,' Leamas said. 'He hopes to meet Mr Thomas this evening.'

'I will tell Mr Thomas,' the girl said. 'Does he know where to meet you?'

'Dolphin Square,' Leamas said. Then he gave the address of Ashe's flat and rang off.

Leamas returned to Ashe's flat. He sat on the camp bed, looking at his hands. After a time he lay down.

As he closed his eyes he remembered Liz lying beside him in the flat in Bayswater. He wondered for a moment what had happened to her.

*

He was woken up by Ashe. With Ashe was a small, plump man, with long grey hair swept back. He spoke with a slight accent. It sounded like a German accent. He said his name was Kiever – Sam Kiever.

They had a gin and tonic. Ashe did most of the talking. He said it was just like old times. They had all night to talk. Kiever said he didn't want to be too late, because he had work to do on the next day.

They agreed to go for a meal at a Chinese restaurant. He knew one opposite Limehouse police station. You had to take your own wine. Ashe just happened to have two bottles of wine in the kitchen. They took that with them and went by taxi.

The dinner was very good. They drank both bottles of wine. After the second bottle Kiever began to talk.

He said he had just come back from West Germany and France. France, he said, was in a hell of a mess. General de Gaulle was finished. When he went no one knew what would happen.

Ashe said, 'What about Germany, Sam? What's happening there?'

Kiever said, 'Germany will be all right if the Yanks can keep control.'

Kiever looked at Leamas, expecting him to say something.

'What do you mean?' Leamas said.

'The Yanks keep changing their minds about Germany,' said Kiever.

'Bloody typical Yanks,' said Leamas.

'Alec doesn't like our American friends,' Ashe said.

This was a clue for Kiever. But Kiever just said, 'Oh really?'

Leamas knew that Kiever was waiting for him to make the first move.

After dinner Ashe said, 'I know a place in Wardour Street. They do you all right there. Shall we go?'

'Just a minute,' said Leamas. 'Just tell me one thing. Who's paying for all this?'

'I am,' said Ashe quickly. 'Sam and I.'

'Well,' said Leamas. 'I haven't got any money to throw away. You know that, don't you?'

'Of course, Alec,' Ashe said. 'I've looked after you up till now, haven't I?'

'Yes,' said Leamas, 'Yes, you have.'

Ashe looked worried. Kiever's face was blank.

13 Kiever Makes an Offer

In the taxi Leamas said nothing. Ashe tried to be friendly. Leamas just shrugged his shoulders. They arrived in Wardour Street and got out of the taxi. Ashe paid the fare.

Ashe then led them down a narrow alley. At the end of the alley was a cheap sign, lit up. It said 'Pussywillow Club. Members only.' On both sides of the door were photos of girls. There was a notice. It said, 'Nature Study. Members only.'

Ashe rang the bell. A very large man in a white shirt and black trousers opened the door.

'I'm a member,' Ashe said. 'These two gentlemen are with me.'

'Let me see your card,' said the large man.

Ashe took a card from his wallet and handed it over.

'Your friends have to pay a pound a head,' said the large man. 'All right?'

He held out the card to Ashe. As he did so Leamas stretched out his hand and took it. Leamas looked at it for a moment. Then he gave it to Ashe.

Leamas then took two pounds from his pocket. He put them into the hand of the man at the door.

They got a table of their own at the back of the room. A two-piece band was playing. Ashe looked at Leamas while they waited for the whisky. Ashe seemed uneasy. Kiever looked bored. The waiter brought a bottle and three glasses.

He poured a little whisky into each glass.

Leamas leaned across the table and said to Ashe, 'Now perhaps you'll tell me what the hell's going on?'

'What do you mean?' said Ashe. 'What *do* you mean, Alec?' Ashe sounded worried.

Leamas said, 'You followed me from prison the day I came out. You told me some damn silly story about meeting me in Berlin. You gave me money which you didn't owe me. You've bought me expensive meals. You're putting me up in your flat.'

Ashe blushed, and said, 'If that's the . . .'

'Don't interrupt,' Leamas said. 'Just damn well wait till I've finished. Do you mind? Your card for this place is made out for a man called Murphy. Is that your name?'

'No,' said Ashe, 'It is not.'

'I suppose you borrowed the card?' said Leamas.

'No, I did not,' said Ashe. 'If you must know, I come here sometimes to find a girl. I used a false name to join the club.'

'Then why,' said Leamas, 'is Murphy the name of the man who owns your flat?'

Kiever finally spoke. He said to Ashe, 'Run on home. I'll look after this.'

*

A girl did a striptease. She was a young, drab girl. She looked poor and sad.

Leamas and Kiever watched in silence.

At last Leamas said, 'I suppose you will say that we saw better shows in Berlin.'

Kiever saw that Leamas was still very angry.

'I expect *you* have,' said Kiever. 'I've often been to Berlin. But I don't like night clubs.'

'Then perhaps you'll tell me why that fellow Ashe picked me up,' Leamas said.

'Yes,' said Kiever. 'I told him to.'

'Why?' said Leamas.

'I am interested in you,' said Kiever. 'I want to make you an offer. I run a newspaper agency. I send articles abroad. It pays well – very well – for interesting stuff.'

'Who publishes it?' said Leamas.

Kiever did not answer, but said, 'A man with your background could make a fortune. Just write some facts about your life. You will have no more worries about money.'

'Who publishes it, Kiever?' asked Leamas.

Leamas sounded angry. For just a moment Kiever looked afraid. But the look passed.

'My clients abroad,' he said. 'I have a man in Paris who publishes a lot of my stuff. Often I don't know who does publish it. And I don't care much.'

Kiever smiled. He said, 'They pay and ask for more. They don't fuss about details. They pay quickly. They pay into foreign banks, so there is no tax to pay.'

Leamas said nothing. He was holding his glass in both hands, staring into it. He knew what Kiever was asking him to do. But he had to pretend to be afraid.

'They would have to pay a hell of a lot,' Leamas said at last.

Kiever gave him some more whisky.

'They are offering fifteen thousand pounds,' said Kiever. 'This will be a first payment. The money is already in a bank in Bern. All you have to do is turn up, prove you are Alec Leamas, and take the money. Then, if you answer questions for one year, you get another five thousand pounds.'

'How soon do you want an answer?' said Leamas.

'Now,' said Kiever. 'You don't have to write anything down. A man will meet you and ask you questions. Someone else will write your answers.'

'Where shall I meet this man?' said Leamas.

'Not in the United Kingdom,' said Kiever. 'It will be safer somewhere abroad. My client said Holland.'

'I haven't got a passport,' Leamas said in a dull voice.

'I have got one for you,' Kiever said smoothly. 'We fly to The Hague tomorrow morning at nine forty-five. Shall we go back to my flat now and talk about it all?'

Kiever paid. They took a taxi to a good address not far from St James's Park.

*

Kiever's flat was expensive. Leamas thought it was just like a hotel room.

'How long have you been here?' said Leamas.

'Not long,' said Kiever, 'a few months, not more.'

'Must cost a lot,' said Leamas. 'Still, I suppose you are

worth it.'

'Thanks,' said Kiever.

There was a bottle of whisky in the room and a soda syphon on a silver-plated tray. At the other end of the room was an archway with a curtain. It led to a bathroom and lavatory.

'Quite a little love nest,' Leamas said. 'All paid for by the great Worker State, I suppose?'

'Shut up,' said Kiever. Then he said, 'If you want me, there is a telephone to my room. I shall be awake.'

'I think I'm old enough to undo my buttons,' Leamas said.

'Then good night,' Kiever said.

He went out of the room.

Leamas said to himself, 'He's nervous, too.'

*

The telephone by his bed woke Leamas. It was Kiever.

'It's six o'clock,' he said. 'Breakfast is at half past.'

'All right,' said Leamas. He had a headache.

*

Kiever must have telephoned for a taxi. At seven o'clock the door-bell rang.

'Got everything?' Kiever said.

'I've no luggage,' Leamas said, 'except a toothbrush and a razor.'

'All that is taken care of,' said Kiever. 'Are you ready?'

'I suppose so,' said Leamas, shrugging his shoulders. 'Have you got a cigarette?'

'No,' said Kiever. 'But you can get some on the plane.'

Kiever gave Leamas a passport.

'You had better look at this,' he said.

It was made out in Leamas' own name with his own photograph in it. It said that Leamas was a clerk, and that he was not married. Leamas held it in his hand. He was nervous. It was like getting married. Whatever was going to happen to him, life would never be the same again.

'What about money?' Leamas said.

'You won't need any,' said Kiever. 'It's all on the firm.'

14 The Mirage

It was cold at the airport. There was a light mist. Everything was damp and grey. The planes were half-hidden in the mist. The airport staff looked cold, and were not very interested in the passengers.

Kiever had brought some luggage for Leamas. They went up to the desk and followed the signs to passport control. Kiever seemed worried about the passport. But Leamas knew that there was nothing wrong with it.

They had twenty minutes to wait. They sat down at a table and ordered coffee.

'And take these things away,' Kiever said to the waiter, pointing to the dirty cups on the table.

'There's a trolley coming round,' the waiter said.

'Take them,' Kiever shouted.

The waiter just turned and walked away. He didn't go to the service counter. He didn't order their coffee.

Kiever was white with anger.

'For God's sake,' said Leamas.'Forget it. Life is too short.'

'Cheeky bastard, that's what he is,' said Kiever.

'All right,' said Leamas, 'make a scene. Then they will never forget us here.'

*

They got through the airport at The Hague with no difficulty. Kiever was not nervous any longer. He talked a lot as they walked from the plane.The Dutch passport officer looked quickly at their passports. 'I hope you enjoy your stay in Holland,' he said.

'Thanks,' said Kiever.

They walked to the main exit. Leamas looked back. He saw a little man in glasses standing at the newspaper counter. He was a worried little man, rather like a frog. He looked like a civil servant or something of the sort.

*

A car was waiting for them in the car park. It was a Volkswagen, with a Dutch number plate. A woman was in the driving seat. They got in. She took no notice of them. She drove off, slowly. She always stopped if the traffic lights were amber; Leamas guessed that she had been told to drive like this. He guessed that they were being followed by another car. He kept looking in the driving mirror to see if he could spot the car, but he could not. Once he saw a black Fiat. But when they went round a corner there was only a van behind them.

Leamas knew The Hague well. He tried to work out where they were going. He guessed they were going north-west. Soon they left the town behind. They came to some large houses which were next to the sand hills along the sea front.

They stopped here. The woman got out and left them in the car. She rang the front door bell of a small cream bungalow. It had a name on a sign hanging from the porch. The name was 'The Mirage.' In the window was a notice. It said, 'No vacancies.'

A plump woman opened the door. 'How nice that you have come,' she said. 'We are so *pleased* that you have come.'

They followed her into the bungalow. Kiever led the way. The driver got back into the car. Leamas looked back down the road along which they had just come. Three hundred yards away was a black car. A Fiat. A man in a raincoat was getting out.

When they were in the hall the woman shook Leamas' hand.

'Welcome!' she said. 'Welcome to "The Mirage". Did you have a good journey?'

'Fine,' said Leamas.

'I'll make your lunch,' she said. 'It is a special lunch. I'll make you something very good. What shall I bring you?'

'Oh, for God's sake,' Leamas said under his breath. Then the door bell rang. The woman went quickly into the kitchen. Kiever opened the front door.

A man came in. He was wearing a mac with leather buttons. He was about as tall as Leamas, but he was older. Leamas thought he was about fifty-five. His face was hard and grey and had deep lines in it. He looked like a soldier.

He held out his hand. 'My name is Peters,' he said. His fingers were slim and polished. 'Did you have a good journey?'

'Yes,' said Kiever, quickly. 'It was very ordinary.'

Then Peters said, 'Mr Leamas and I have a lot to talk about. I do not think you need stay, Sam. You could take the Volkswagen back to town.'

Kiever smiled. Leamas saw that he was glad to go.

'Goodbye, Leamas,' said Kiever. He sounded in a good mood. 'Good luck, old man.'

Leamas nodded, but took no notice when Kiever tried to shake hands.

'Goodbye,' Kiever said again.

Then he let himself quietly out of the front door.

Leamas followed Peters into the back room. There were heavy lace curtains at the window. The window-sill was covered with potted plants.

The furniture in the room was heavy, old and cheap. In the middle of the room was a table with two chairs.

The table was covered with a rust coloured table-cloth. It looked more like a carpet than a tablecloth.

'Look,' Leamas said, 'Just forget all this kindness. Do

you understand? We both know what we are after. You've got a paid traitor. Good luck to you. For God's sake don't pretend you love me.'

He sounded afraid.

Peters nodded.

'Kiever told me you were proud,' he said. Then he said, without a smile, 'Only proud men beat up shop-keepers.'

Leamas guessed Peters was a Russian. But he wasn't sure. Peters' English was nearly perfect.

They sat at the table.

'Did Kiever say what I am going to pay you?' Peters said.

'Yes,' said Leamas. 'Fifteen thousand pounds from a bank in Bern.'

'Yes,' said Peters.

'He said you might want to ask me more questions during the next year,' said Leamas. 'I would get another five thousand pounds if I kept myself on hand to do that.'

Peters nodded.

'I will not do that,' said Leamas. 'It would not work. You know that as well as I do. I want to get the fifteen thousand pounds and get clear. Your people are hard on traitors. So is our side.'

Peters nodded again.

'You could, of course, come somewhere safer,' he said.

'Behind the Iron Curtain?' asked Leamas.

'Yes,' said Peters.

Leamas shook his head. Then he said,

'You will need about three days to ask me your first set of questions. Then you'll have to ask me some more to check the details. Is that right?'

'Not really,' said Peters.

Leamas looked up at him with interest.

'I see,' said Leamas. 'They've sent an expert, have they? Or isn't Moscow in on all this?'

Peters was silent. He just looked at Leamas, summing him up. At last he picked up the pencil in front of him and said,

'Shall we begin? First your war service. What did you do in the war?'

Leamas shrugged.

'Start with the war, if you want to,' he said. 'It's up to you.'

'That's right,' said Peters. 'We'll begin with your war service. Just talk.'

15 Leamas Tells All

'I joined the army in 1939,' Leamas began. 'I was in the Engineers. Then they wanted men who could speak foreign languages to go abroad. I could speak Dutch, German, and French. I was fed up with the Engineers, so I asked to go abroad. I knew Holland well. My father had a machine-tool factory there, in the town of Leiden. I had lived there for nine years.

'After training me to be a spy, they sent me to Holland. I stayed there for two years. Holland is a hard country for a spy. There is nowhere to hide. It's all so flat with no rough country. We lost spies quicker than we could find them.

'In 1943 I got out of Holland. I went back to England for a few months, then off to Norway. That was a picnic. In 1945 they paid me off. I came back to Holland to join my father. That did not work so I joined a friend in Bristol. He was a travel agent and we worked together. But the business failed after eighteen months.

'Then, out of the blue, I got a letter from the London Spy-Agency. They asked if I would like to join them again. I did not really want to. I had had enough of spying. So I said that I would think about it. About a year later I wrote to them and said that I would join them again. By the end of 1949 they had signed me on. Am I going too fast?'

'No,' said Peters. He poured himself some whisky. 'I shall have to check it, of course. And I shall want some names and dates.'

There was a knock at the door. The woman came in with lunch. It was a huge meal of cold meats, bread and soup. Peters pushed his notes aside. They ate in silence.

Leamas knew that the cross examination had begun.

*

Lunch was cleared away.

Peters said, 'So you went back to headquarters?'

'Yes,' said Leamas. 'For a while they gave me a desk job in the office. I had to help work out how big the armies were in Iron Curtain countries.'

'Which section were you in?' said Peters.

'Number four,' said Leamas. 'I was there from February 1950 until May 1951. Then I was sent to Berlin.'

'In 1954 we had our first big success,' Leamas said. 'Fritz Feger began to give us information. He was second man in the East German Defence Ministry. He was quite a catch. Up till then it had been hard work. He worked for us for two years. Then, one day, we heard no more. I hear that he died in prison. It was another three years before we found another man. In 1959 Karl Riemeck turned up. Karl was a top man in the East German Communist Party. He was a member of the Council. He was the best spy I ever had.'

'He is now dead,' Peters said.

Leamas looked ashamed.

'I was there when he was shot,' Leamas said. 'He had a woman who came across the border just before he died. He had told her everything. She knew the whole damned story. No wonder he was killed!'

Peters said, 'Let's say no more about Berlin. We'll

come back to that later. Tell me this. When Karl died you flew back to London, didn't you? Did you stay in London then?'

'Yes,' said Leamas.

'What job did you do?' said Peters.

'I was in headquarters,' said Leamas, 'in the banking section. I helped to send pay out to spies in other countries.'

'Did you deal with the spies yourself?' said Peters.

'Of course not,' said Leamas. 'We just sent money out to a foreign bank. The spy would pick it up from there.'

'How did you describe your spies?' Peters said. 'Did you give them other names?'

'No,' said Leamas. 'We used numbers. Every area was given a number. Every spy then used his area number plus his own code. Karl Riemeck's number was 8 A/l.'

Leamas was sweating. Peters was watching him closely, as one gambler watches another across the table. Peters wondered what would break Leamas. Would Leamas keep his best information till last? Peters did not think so. He saw that Leamas was a proud man. He would tell some lies. Peters knew that he would have to find those lies and sort them out.

'I think,' Peters said, 'that we will go over your work in Berlin now. Could we start with 1951 and go on to 1961?'

*

Leamas watched Peters take a cigarette from the box on the table. Leamas noticed two things. Peters was left-handed. He put the cigarette in his mouth with the maker's name away from him, so that it burnt first. Leamas liked this about Peters. He thought Peters was a man like himself.

Peters had an odd face. It was dull and grey. He looked as if he had been in prison. Nothing would ever change his face now. His hair was stiff and grey. Leamas wondered if Peters was his real name and if he was married. He looked a strong man, not a bit like Ashe or Kiever. Leamas knew that Kiever was more important than Ashe. Now Peters was more important than Kiever.

Leamas began to talk about Berlin. Peters did not stop him often. If he did stop Leamas, he asked good questions. Leamas liked him for this.

Leamas told Peters that it had taken a long time to get any success in East Berlin. There were lots of spies working. But most of them were second-rate. The only good man had been Feger in 1954. And he had spoiled them by being too good. When he died it was worse than before. Then Karl Riemeck had come.

Peters was interested in the story of Karl.

Leamas said, 'One of our men was called de Jong. One day he went for a picnic in the woods on the edge of East Berlin. He parked his car, locked, in a rough road near a canal. After the picnic his children had run back to the car. When they reached the car they stopped. Then they ran back. They told de Jong that somebody had forced open the car door. The handle was broken and the door was open. De Jong thought it had been forced by a piece of steel tube. He swore. He had left his camera in the car. But the camera was still there, so was his coat. But on the driving seat was a tobacco tin. Inside the tin was a film cartridge. It was from a mini-camera.

'De Jong drove home. He developed the film. It contained the notes of the last secret meeting of the Council of the East German Communist Party. De Jong was able to get proof that the notes were the real thing.'

Leamas went on,

'I took over then. I needed some success. I had done nothing since coming to Berlin.

'Exactly a week later I took de Jong's car to the same

place and went for a walk. I walked in the woods. It was a deserted place. I did not watch the car. I was afraid if I did I might frighten him off.

'Then I went back to the car. There was nothing there. I was a damned fool to expect anything. The Communist Party Council had not met since de Jong's picnic. It was not due to meet for another two weeks.

'In two weeks' time I took de Jong's car again. This time I took a thousand dollars in a picnic case. I left the car unlocked for two hours. When I came back there was a tobacco tin on the driving seat. The picnic case had gone.

'The films were full of very good stuff. In the next six weeks I did it twice. The same thing happened each time.

'I knew I had hit a gold mine,' Leamas said. 'I did not want headquarters to find out. And so I sent them a false report. I did not want them to take this case from me. It was my only chance to show them that I could succeed. Headquarters would have messed it all up.

'I worked like a madman for three weeks. I was trying to find out who was working for me. I made lists of all the Communists who went to the secret meetings. I had thirty-one names on my list. It could be any one of them.

'Then I looked at the films again,' Leamas said. 'I noticed that the pages of the notes had no numbers. On some pages there were figures crossed out. This puzzled me. Then I understood. These were the first copies of the notes. And only the very top man saw them. I had nearly found my man.

'I went back to my list, and found one man; Karl Riemeck was his name. He had been a prisoner of war in England, for three years. His sister had lived in Pomerania. The Russians invaded Pomerania and he had never heard of his sister since.

'I decided to take a chance. I found out that Karl Riemeck's prisoner of war number had been 29012. I bought an East German children's book of science fiction. Then I wrote in it, "This book belongs to Carla Riemeck, signed Moonspacewoman 29012." Then, underneath, I wrote, "Anybody who wants to fly in a space ship should sign this form." I put in a sheet of paper for the names.

'I took de Jong's car to the usual place and left the book on the seat. 'When I came back the book was gone. There was a tobacco tin on the seat. In it were three rolls of film. One roll of film showed the whole East German Spy Service.'

Peters said, 'Just a minute. Do you mean that Riemeck sent you all this?'

'Yes,' Leamas said.

'It's not possible,' said Peters. 'He must have had help.'

'He did, later on,' said Leamas. 'I am coming to that.'

'I know what you are going to say,' said Peters. 'He got others to work for him. But he must have had help from *above* as well. One of his bosses must have been in on it.'

'No,' said Leamas. 'I never thought that.'

'Don't you think so now?' said Peters.

'No,' said Leamas.

'When you sent this stuff to headquarters,' Peters said, 'didn't they think it was too much for just one man?'

'No,' said Leamas.

'Strange,' said Peters. 'But do go on.'

'I drove back to the same place a week later,' said Leamas. 'I was nervous. When I got there, I saw three bicycles lying in the grass. Two hundred yards away were three men fishing in the canal. I got out of the car as usual and began to walk. I had gone about twenty yards when I heard a shout. I looked round. One of the men was waving at me. The other two were watching me too. I was wearing an old mac. I had my hands in my pockets. It was too late to take them out. I knew that the two men on the side were covering the man in the middle. If I took my hands out of my pockets they would shoot me. I stopped ten yards away from the middle man.

' "You want something?" I said.

' "Are you Leamas?" the man said. He was small and plump and he spoke English.

' "I am Leamas," I said.

' "What is your identity number?" he said.

'"PRT/L58003/1," I said.

' "Let's go for a walk, Mr Leamas," he said. "Take your mac off. You won't need that. My friends here will look after it for you."

'I took it off. Then we walked quickly away towards the wood.'

*

'You know as well as I do who he was,' Leamas said to Peters. 'He was Karl Riemeck, the third most important man in the Ministry and the man whose job it was to make notes at the top level Communist secret meetings.'

'But he could not have seen all those papers,' said Peters. 'They would never let one man see so much.'

Leamas shrugged his shoulders.

'They did,' he said.

'What did he do with his money?' Peters said.

'I didn't give him any more after that day,' Leamas said. 'Headquarters took it over from then. It was paid into a West German bank. He often gave me back what I had given him. London banked it for him.'

'How much did you tell headquarters?' Peters asked.

'Everything,' said Leamas. 'I had to. Then they told everybody. Then it was only a matter of time before it was all over. Headquarters got greedy. They wanted more. We had to tell Karl to get more men to work for him. He did. It was damned silly. It made life dangerous for him. It was the beginning of the end.'

'How much did you get out of him?' said Peters.

'How much?' said Leamas. 'I don't know. It lasted a hell of a time. I think they had suspected him before the end. Some of his last stuff was pretty poor. I think they kept him away from the good stuff.'

'Exactly what did he give you?' said Peters.

Leamas told Peters everything. Peters noticed how good Leamas' memory was. He could remember everything, all the dates, the sums of money, all the names.

'I'm sorry,' Peters said. 'But I can't believe that one man could have given you so much.'

'He *was* able,' said Leamas, suddenly angry. 'He damn well did, and that's all there is to it.'

'Didn't headquarters ask you to find out how he got the stuff?' asked Peters.

'No,' snapped Leamas. 'Riemeck was touchy about that. Headquarters decided not to bother.'

They said no more about Karl Riemeck. But Leamas told Peters about his other spies. He told him also about his Berlin office, his staff, all about the flat they used. They talked into the night, then all through the next day. At last Leamas stumbled into bed. He knew he had given all he knew about the West's spy work in Berlin. He had drunk two bottles of whisky in two days.

*

One thing puzzled Leamas. Peters had been sure that Karl Riemeck had help. Leamas remembered that the Chief had asked him about this at headquarters. It was clear that Peters and the Chief both thought that someone else had helped Riemeck.

Perhaps it was true. Perhaps there was somebody else. Perhaps this was the man the Chief wanted to save from Mundt.

Anyway, tomorrow would tell. Tomorrow Leamas would tell everything.

16 The Second Day

Peters came back at eight o'clock the next morning. They sat down at the table and began.

'So you came back to London,' Peters said. 'What did you do there?'

'They put me on the shelf,' said Leamas. 'I knew I was finished when that fool met me at the airport. I went straight to headquarters to tell the Chief about Karl's death.'

'What did they do with you?' said Peters.

'At first they told me to hang around,' Leamas said. 'They said that I would soon get a pension. They tried to be kind. I got angry. They put me in banking section at headquarters, with a lot of women. I can't remember much about that. I started to drink a lot. I went through a bit of a bad patch.'

He lit a cigarette. Peters nodded.

'That was why they kicked me out,' Leamas said. 'They didn't like me drinking.'

'Tell me all you *do* remember about the banking section,' Peters said.

'It was dull,' said Leamas. 'I am not made for desk work. That's why I stayed so long in Berlin. I knew that they would put me on the shelf when I came home.'

'What did you do?' said Peters.

Leamas shrugged.

'I sat on my behind in the same room as a couple of women,' Leamas said. 'We just filled in forms. The finance section used to send us the forms. We would fill them in. I used to sign some cheques or get the bank to send some money on.'

Leamas went on, 'Then I remember a thing called "Rolling Stone". This was a code name. I used to take money abroad and drop it at banks for a spy. I got two trips like this, one to Copenhagen, one to Helsinki.'

'How much did you take?' said Peters.

'Ten thousand dollars to Copenhagen,' Leamas said. 'Forty thousand D-marks to Helsinki.'

Peters put down his pencil.

'Who was that money for?' he said.

'God knows,' said Leamas. 'I used a false passport and just put the money into the foreign banks. The spy then used a false bank book to take the money out again.'

Leamas listened to himself saying this. It sounded a very unlikely story.

'What was the code name?' said Peters.

'I told you,' said Leamas, 'Rolling Stone. I think we got the idea from the Russians. It was a very hard thing to work out. I used a different name on each trip.'

That will please him, Leamas thought.

'When did you go on your trips?' said Peters.

'Copenhagen on the fifteenth of June,' said Leamas. 'I flew back the same night. Helsinki at the end of September. I stayed there two nights. I had a bit of fun in Helsinki.'

Leamas grinned at Peters, but Peters took no notice.

Peters was writing all the time now. Leamas guessed there was a tape recorder hidden in the room. He also guessed that Peters would send this report to Moscow later that day.

'Tell me,' said Peters, 'what did you make out of this for yourself?'

'Nothing,' said Leamas. 'I thought it was too clever. Why couldn't they just meet the spy and give him the money? I didn't like it.'

'I see,' said Peters. 'What names did you use in Copenhagen and Helsinki?'

'In Copenhagen I used the name Robert Lang,' Leamas said.

'When exactly were you in Copenhagen?' said

Peters.

'I told you,' said Leamas, 'June the fifteenth. I got there in the morning at about 11.30.'

'Which bank did you use?' said Peters.

'Oh, for God's sake,' said Leamas, angrily. 'The Royal Scandinavian. I've told you all this.'

'I just wanted to make sure,' said Peters calmly. 'What name did you use in Helsinki?'

'Stephen Bennett,' said Leamas, 'I was there at the end of September.'

Leamas got up. He went to the sideboard and poured himself some whisky. He did not bother about Peters.

'You are a very proud man, Leamas,' Peters said again.

Peters left soon after that. He said good day to Leamas and walked down the road along the sea front. It was lunchtime.

17 The Third Day

Peters did not come back that afternoon. Nor did he come the next morning. Leamas stayed in waiting. He was getting annoyed. He asked the housekeeper when Peters would be back. She just smiled and shrugged her shoulders. At about eleven o'clock the next morning he went for a walk along the sea front. He bought some cigarettes and stared at the sea.

There was a girl standing on the beach. She was throwing bread to the seagulls. She had her back to him. The sea wind was blowing her long black hair. It pulled at her coat. Her body looked like a bow. She made Leamas think of Liz. He knew he must get home quickly to Liz. A week, two weeks perhaps, and he would be home. He would have plenty of money. The Chief said he could keep what they paid. That would be enough. He would have fifteen thousand pounds and a pension from headquarters. That would be enough for him to come in from the cold.

He walked back to the bungalow. It was a quarter to twelve. The woman let him in. She said nothing to him. But when he had gone into the back room he heard her lift the phone and dial a number. She only spoke for a few seconds. At half past twelve she brought him his lunch, and some English newspapers.

He enjoyed reading the newspapers until three o'clock. He read them slowly and carefully.

At three o'clock Peters came back. As soon as Leamas saw him he knew something was wrong. They did not sit at the table. Peters did not take off his mac.

'I've got bad news for you,' Peters said. 'They are watching the ports.'

Leamas said, 'What do they want me for?'

'They want you for not going to a police station after coming out of prison,' said Peters. 'At least, that is what they say.'

'Why do they really want me?' said Leamas.

'The word is going round that you have given away State secrets,' said Peters. 'Your photo is in all the London evening papers.'

The Chief had done it. He must have started it all. Ashe and Kiever might have talked. 'But the Chief could still have stopped this happening,' Leamas said to himself, 'and the Chief told me that it would be over in a couple of weeks. "You will be home in a couple of weeks," he told me. "You will have to lie low when you come back, but it will not be for long. I have agreed to pay you until Mundt is finished."'

And now this.

This wasn't part of the plan. This was different. What the hell was he supposed to do? If he pulled out now he would spoil it all. He would have to go with Peters if Peters asked him to. But where to? It might be to Poland or Czechoslovakia or God knows where. If he went, they might never let him out again. Even if Peters was lying to test him, he would still have to go, or he would fail the test.

For the first time since it all began Leamas was afraid.

The Chief had done it. Leamas was sure. The Chief had been too kind to be true. He had known this all the time. The money was a warning. Leamas should have seen that something was wrong when the Chief had said he could keep the money.

'Now how the devil did they get on to it?' Leamas said quietly. 'I suppose Ashe told them, or Kiever.'

'It is possible,' said Peters. 'Anything is possible in this job. Every country in the West is looking for you.'

'You've got me on the hook, haven't you, Peters,' Leamas said. 'Your side must be laughing. Or did they give the tip-off themselves?'

'Let's stick to what we know,' said Peters. 'Everyone is looking for you. It doesn't matter how they know.'

'Have you brought the London papers with you?' said Leamas.

'Of course not,' said Peters. 'We cannot get them here. We got a telegram from London.'

'That's a lie,' said Leamas. 'You can only talk to your headquarters.'

'Not this time,' said Peters. 'I used a direct link.'

'Well, well,' said Leamas. 'You must be important!'

'You know your choice,' said Peters. 'Either you let us look after you, or you look after yourself. But you've got no false papers, no money, nothing. Your British passport will run out in ten days.'

'Why not give me a Swiss passport,' said Leamas, 'and some money and let me run. I can look after myself.'

'I'm afraid I cannot do that,' said Peters.

'You mean you haven't finished asking me questions,' said Leamas.

'That's right,' said Peters.

50

'When you've finished with the questions,' said Leamas, 'what will you do with me?'

Peters shrugged. 'What do you suggest?' he said.

'A new passport,' said Leamas, 'and some money.'

'I will ask my bosses,' said Peters. 'Are you coming with me?'

Leamas didn't answer. Then he smiled and said, 'If I didn't what would you do? I've got quite a story to tell, haven't I?'

'I am going tonight,' Peters said.

Leamas went to the window. A storm was gathering over the North Sea. He watched the gulls and the dark clouds. The girl had gone.

'All right,' he said at last. 'Fix it up.'

'There's no plane East until tomorrow,' Peters said. 'There's a plane to Berlin in an hour. We shall take that. It's going to be very close.'

Leamas was frightened.

18 Friends of Alec

The men called on Liz the same evening.

She thought they were too smart to be policemen. They came in a small black car with an aerial on it. One was short and plump. He had glasses and wore odd, expensive clothes. He was a kind, worried little man. Liz trusted him. She did not know why.

The other man was smoother. He was rather like a boy. They said they came from Special Branch. They had printed cards and photos. The plump one did most of the talking.

'I think you were friendly with Alec Leamas,' he said.

'Yes,' Liz said. 'How did you know?'

'We found out by chance the other day,' the plump man said. 'When you go to prison you have to give the

51

name of your next of kin. Leamas said he did not have any. That was a lie as a matter of fact. They asked him whom they should tell if anything went wrong in prison. He said you.'

'I see,' Liz said.

'Does anyone else know you were friendly with him?' the plump man said.

'No,' said Liz.

'Did you go to the court after he had hit the grocer?' asked the plump man.

'No,' said Liz.

'Nobody has come to see you?' the plump man said. 'No press, no one at all?'

'No,' said Liz, 'I've told you. No one else knew.'

The little man looked closely at her for a moment. Then he asked:

'Did it surprise you when Leamas beat up the grocer?'

'Yes,' said Liz, 'Of course.'

'Why did he do it?' said the little man.

'I don't know,' said Liz. 'Because the grocer would not give him credit, I suppose. But I think he always meant to.'

She wondered if she was saying too much. But she longed to talk to somebody about it. She was so lonely. She did not think there was any harm.

'That night,' she said, 'the night before he did it, we talked together. We had supper, a sort of special one. I knew it was our last night. Alec got a bottle of red wine from somewhere. I didn't like it much. Alec drank most of it. Then I asked him, "Is this goodbye?"'

'What did he say?' said the little man.

'He said he had a job to do,' said Liz. 'I didn't really understand him. Not really.'

There was a long silence. The little man looked very worried. Then he said,

'Do you believe that?'

'I don't know,' said Liz. She was terrified for Alec.

She didn't know why.

'Leamas has got two children,' said the little man. 'Did he tell you that? He is divorced.'

Liz said nothing.

'But he gave *your* name as his next of kin,' the little man said. 'Why do you think he did that?'

Liz blushed.

'I was in love with him,' she said.

'Was he in love with you?' the little man said.

'Perhaps,' Liz said, 'I don't know.'

'Are you still in love with him?' the little man said.

'Yes,' said Liz.

'Did he ever say he would come back?' said the little man.

'No,' said Liz.

'Did he say goodbye to you?' the little man said. 'Tell us anything else he said. Anything. Tell us, for Alec's sake.'

Liz shook her head.

'Please go,' she said. 'Please don't ask any more questions. Please go now.'

When the older man got to the door, he stopped. He took a card from his wallet. He put it on the table, quietly. Liz thought he was a very shy man.

'If ever you want help, ring me up. If anything happens about Leamas, please tell me,' he said. 'Do you understand?'

'Who are you?' Liz said.

'I am a friend of Alec Leamas,' he said. 'Another thing. One last question. Did Alec know you were a Communist?'

'Yes,' she said. 'I told him.'

'Does the Communist Party know about you and Alec?' the plump man said.

'I have told you,' she said. 'No one knew.'

Then she cried out, white faced,

'Where is he? Tell where he is. Why don't you tell me where he is? I can help him. Can't you see? I'll look

53

after him. Even if he's gone mad, I don't care. I swear I don't. I wrote to him in prison. I know I shouldn't. I just told him he could come back any time. I shall always wait for him.'

She couldn't speak any more. She just sobbed and sobbed. She stood in the middle of the room, sobbing. She buried her face in her hands. The little man watched her.

'He's gone abroad,' the little man said quietly. 'We don't quite know where he is. He isn't mad. But he should not have said all that to you. It was a pity.'

The younger man said:

'We will look after you. We'll give you money and that kind of thing.'

'Who are you?' Liz said again.

'Friends of Alec,' they said. 'Good friends.'

She heard them go quietly down the stairs. They went into the street. She watched them from her window. They got into the small black car and drove away towards the park.

Then she remembered the card. She went to the table. She picked it up and held it to the light. It was an expensive card. There was no police station or anything. Just the name.

The name was Smiley. Mr George Smiley, 9 Bywater Street, Chelsea. Then the telephone number underneath.

It was very strange.

19 Leamas Goes East

Leamas walked to the plane. He was on his way to Berlin. Suddenly he felt afraid. He knew he was slowing down. The Chief was right. He was slowing down.

Leamas had known this for some time. He remembered the time he had tried to meet Karl Riemeck. Karl had sent a message. He had something special for Leamas.

Leamas had driven at seventy kilometres an hour along the motorway. He took risks to beat the clock. He drove fast in and out of the traffic.

A small car had turned out into the fast lane in front of Leamas. Leamas stamped on the brake. He turned his lights full on and sounded his horn. He just missed it by a split second. As he passed the car he saw four children in the back. They were waving and laughing. He saw the father's face. He was very frightened.

Leamas had driven on, cursing. Then, suddenly, he felt afraid. His hands shook. His face was hot. His heart was beating fast. He pulled off the road into a lay-by. He got out of the car and stood watching the heavy lorries rushing past. He thought of the little car and the children. He thought how it would look if it was crushed by the lorries. He thought of the children and how their bodies would be thrown on the road.

Leamas drove very slowly after that. He missed his meeting with Karl. He never drove after that without remembering how he had just missed that little car and the children.

Leamas thought about the car and the children as he got onto the plane. The plane took off.

He undid his seatbelt. He felt suddenly afraid.

He wondered what would happen to him. The Chief hadn't talked about it. All the Chief had said was that he had to kill Mundt.

Leamas thought about torture. He didn't think he could stand it. He had read books about it. He had read how spies had tried to get themselves used to pain by holding lighted matches to their fingers. He hadn't read much, but he remembered that.

*

It was nearly dark when they landed at Berlin airport. Leamas watched the lights of Berlin rise to meet them. He felt the thud as the plane landed. He saw the Customs men come out.

Leamas was worried. He had lived in Berlin for a long time. He was afraid someone at the airport would know him. He walked with Peters along the endless corridors. Still he did not see anyone he knew. Then he realised that he was really hoping he would see someone he knew.

They were walking through the main hall. Suddenly Peters stopped. He seemed to change his mind. He took Leamas to a small side door. He opened it and they were in a car park. Peters stopped underneath the light. He put his case on the ground. Then he took his newspaper from under his arm. He folded it and pushed it into the left pocket of his mac. Then he picked up his case again. A pair of headlights came on from one of the cars in the car park. Then they were dipped. Then they were off.

'Come on,' Peters said. He walked quickly across the car park. Leamas followed slowly. They reached the first row of cars. The back door of a black Mercedes opened from the inside.

*

It was an old Mercedes 180. Leamas got in without saying anything. Peters sat beside him in the back. They pulled away and overtook a small DKW. Two men were sitting in the front of the DKW. Twenty yards down the road there was a phone box. A man was in it. He watched them go by. He was talking into the phone. Leamas looked out of the back window of the Mercedes. The DKW was following them. Quite a party, he thought.

It was easy crossing the border into East Berlin. Leamas did not think it would be so easy. They went slowly for ten minutes. Leamas guessed they had to go across the border at a set time. They got near the border. The DKW car overtook them and stopped at the police hut. The Mercedes hung back. Two minutes later the red and white barrier went up. As it did so both cars drove over together. The Mercedes went over in second gear. Its engine screamed. The driver pressed himself back against his seat.

Leamas looked out. He could just see the Eastern side of the wall. The forts on the wall looked like dragon's teeth. There was a double fence of barbed wire.

'Where are we going?' Leamas said.

'We are there,' Peters said. 'We are in the German Democratic Republic. They are going to let you stay here.'

'I thought we would be going further East,' said Leamas.

'We are,' Peters said. 'We shall stay here a day or two first. The Germans want to talk with you.'

'I see,' said Leamas.

'I have told them about you,' Peters said.

'And they asked to see me?' Leamas said.

'They have never met anyone like you,' said Peters. 'You know so much about the other side.'

'Where will we go from Germany?' Leamas said.

'East again,' said Peters.

'Who will I see in Germany?' Leamas asked.

'Does it matter?' said Peters.

'Not much,' Leamas said. 'I know most of their names. I just wondered who it would be.'

'Who do you think it will be?' Peters said.

'Fiedler,' said Leamas. 'Mundt's man Fiedler. He does all the big jobs. He's a bastard.'

'Why?' said Peters.

'He's a savage,' said Leamas. 'I have heard about him. He caught one of our spies and nearly killed him.'

'Spying is not like a game of cricket,' Peters said.

Then they sat in silence. So it was Fiedler, Leamas thought.

Leamas knew Fiedler. He had seen his photograph. He was a slim, neat man. He was quite young and had a smooth face. His hair was dark and he had bright brown eyes. He was clever and savage. He seemed happy to be second to Mundt. He was a lonely man. No one liked him. No one trusted him.

The Chief had told Leamas about Fiedler.

'We must use Fiedler,' the Chief had said. 'He's the only man who is clever enough to get Mundt. He hates Mundt's guts. Fiedler is a Jew. Mundt hates Jews. We have already given Fiedler something to help him against Mundt. You must play your part to get him to use it. Of course you'll never meet Fiedler. At least I hope you won't.'

The Chief laughed when he said this. It seemed a good joke then. At least it was for the Chief.

*

The car drove on. It must have been past midnight. They drove along an unmade road.

Now they stopped. The DKW drew up beside them. Leamas and Peters got out of the Mercedes. They saw that there were now three people in the other car. Two got out. The other sat in the back. He was reading some papers by the light from the car roof.

They had parked by some unused stables. Leamas saw a low farm-house. It had walls of wood and white brick. The moon was up. It shone brightly. They could see the dark hills. They walked to the house. Peters and Leamas walked in front. The other two men came behind. The third man still sat in the DKW, reading.

They reached the door. Peters stopped. They waited for the other two men to catch them up. One of the men carried a bunch of keys. The other man kept his hands in his pockets. He had a gun. He was covering Leamas and Peters.

'They are taking no chances,' Leamas said. 'What do

they think I am?'

'They are not paid to think,' Peters said.

Peters turned to the men. He said, 'Is he coming?'

'He'll come,' said the man. 'He likes to come on his own.'

They went into the house. It was like a hunting lodge. It was badly lit, with pale lights. It was like a deserted house. In the drawing-room there was dark heavy furniture. There were the usual photographs of Russian leaders.

Peters sat down. Leamas did the same. They waited for ten minutes, perhaps longer. Then Peters spoke to one of the two men.

'Go and tell him we're waiting,' he said. 'And find us some food. We're hungry.'

The man went towards the door.

'And whisky,' Peters said. 'Tell them to bring whisky and some glasses.'

The man shrugged his heavy shoulders. He went out, leaving the door open behind him.

'Have you been here before?' Leamas said to Peters.

'Yes,' said Peters, 'many times.'

'What for?' said Leamas.

'This kind of thing,' Peters said. 'Not quite the same as this. But our sort of work.'

'With Fiedler?' Leamas asked.

'Yes,' Peters said.

'Is he good?' Leamas said.

'Not bad for a Jew,' Peters said.

Leamas heard a sound at the other end of the room. He turned and saw Fiedler, standing in the doorway. In one hand he held a bottle of whisky. In the other hand he had glasses and some water. He was no more than five foot six tall. He wore a dark suit. The jacket was too long. He looked a bit like an animal.

'Hello,' Fiedler said to Leamas. 'Glad to see you.'

'Hello, Fiedler,' Leamas said.

'You've reached the end of the road,' Fiedler said.

'What the hell do you mean?' said Leamas.

'I mean that you are not going further East,' Fiedler said. 'Sorry.'

Leamas turned to Peters.

'Is this true?' he said. Leamas was shaking with anger. 'Is it true?' he said. 'Tell me.'

Peters nodded. 'Yes,' he said. 'I am the go-between. We had to do it this way. I'm sorry,' he said.

'We had to bring you here,' Fiedler said.

'You bastard,' Leamas said. 'Why did you have to use a Russian?'

'We didn't know that your own people in England would find out about you so quickly,' Fiedler said.

'No?' said Leamas. 'But you told them, didn't you? Isn't that what happened? Well, isn't it?'

The Chief had told Leamas to pretend to hate them. The Chief had said, 'They will expect that. Pretend to hate them. Then they will think what you say is true.'

'That is a silly thing to say,' Fiedler said. 'Why should we tell your side about you?'

Then Fiedler said something to Peters in Russian. Peters nodded and stood up.

'Goodbye,' he said to Leamas. 'Good luck.'

Peters then walked over to the door. As he got there he turned and again said to Leamas, 'Good luck.'

Leamas went very pale. He held his hands loosely across his body. He looked as if he was ready for a fight.

Peters stayed near the door.

Then Leamas said, 'I should have known. I should have guessed, Fiedler, that you would get the Russian to do your dirty work for you. You haven't got the guts to do it yourself.'

Leamas' voice sounded very odd. It was like the voice of a very angry man.

'I know you, Fiedler,' Leamas went on. 'You were in Canada in the war. That was a damn good place to be. I bet you put your fat head in Mummy's apron when a plane went over. What are you now? You're just Mundt's little servant. Well, I pity you, Fiedler. One day Mundt will finish you off. Then your Mummy won't help you.'

Fiedler shrugged.

'Just get it over, Leamas,' he said. 'Pretend you are going to the dentist. The sooner it's all over, the sooner you can go home. Have some food and go to bed now.'

'You know damned well I can't go back home now,' Leamas said. 'You've seen to that. You've finished me. You knew damned well I would not come here unless I had to.'

Fiedler looked at his thin, strong fingers.

'This is not the time to talk like that,' he said. 'But you can't complain. You know the sort of work spies do. You don't matter. I don't matter. Our countries use us and then forget us.'

Leamas was watching Fiedler as though he hated him.

'I know your set-up,' Leamas said. 'They say you want Mundt's job. I suppose you'll get it now. It's time Mundt finished. Perhaps this is it.'

'I don't understand,' Fiedler said.

'I'm your big success, aren't I,' Leamas said.

Fiedler thought for a moment. Then he said, 'Well, we got you, didn't we? I don't know if you were worth it. We shall see. But it was a good job.'

Then Fiedler sat on the arm of the sofa. He looked hard at Leamas.

Then he said, 'You are right to be angry. Who told your people we had got you? We didn't. You may not believe that, but it is true. So who told them? You had no friends. You had no address. You were just drifting around. Then how the devil did they know you had gone? Someone told them. It wasn't Ashe or Kiever. They are both under arrest.'

'Under arrest?' Leamas said.

'Yes, they were mixed up in one or two other things,'

said Fiedler. 'If you had told us everything in Holland, you could have gone. Peters would have given you the money and let you go. But you haven't told us everything. And I want to know everything.'

'Well, you've made a mistake,' Leamas said. 'I know damn all.'

There was a silence. Peters nodded at Fiedler. It was not a friendly nod. Then Peters went out of the room.

*

The guards showed Leamas to his bedroom. They walked down a wide corridor. They came to a double door. It was painted dark green. One of the guards unlocked it. They told Leamas to go first. He pushed the door open. He was in a small room like a cell. It had two bunk beds, a chair and a simple desk. It was like being in a prison camp. There were pictures of girls on the walls. All the windows had bars. At the far end of the room was another door. They told Leamas to go on. He put down his bags and went through the door. There was another room, exactly like the first one. But there was only one bed and the walls were bare. This was his room.

'You bring those bags,' he said. 'I'm tired.'

He lay on the bed, with all his clothes on. In a few minutes he was fast asleep.

20 More Questions

A sentry woke Leamas with his breakfast. It was black bread and coffee. He got out of bed and went to the window.

He dressed slowly. The coffee was sour. He was just going to start eating when Fiedler came into the room.

'Good morning,' Fiedler said cheerfully. 'Don't stop eating.'

Fiedler sat down on the bed. Leamas said to himself. 'This man has got guts. You've got to give him that.'

'You are a problem,' Fiedler said.

'I don't see that,' Leamas said. 'I've told you all I know.'

Fiedler smiled. 'Oh no,' he said. 'Oh no, you haven't. You've told us what you *know* we know.'

'Damned clever,' Leamas said. He pushed his food away and lit a cigarette. His last.

'Let me ask you a question,' Fiedler said. 'You are a spy. Now, what would *you* do if you had found out what we have found out from you?'

'What have I told you?' Leamas said.

'My dear Leamas,' Fiedler said, 'you've only told us one thing. We know all about Karl Riemeck. We knew all about your work in Berlin. You have not told us anything we did not know about that. But you haven't told us anything worth fifteen thousand pounds. Oh no.'

'Listen,' Leamas said. 'I didn't want to meet you. You, Kiever and Peters set it up. You started it all. You came after me. You set the price. You took the risk. Don't blame me, if it's a flop.'

That will make them wonder, Leamas thought.

'It's not a flop,' Fiedler said. 'It isn't over yet. You've only told us one new thing. I mean your "Rolling Stone" story.*   Now, what would *you* do if I had told *you* a story like that?'

Leamas shrugged.

'Tell me,' Fiedler said, 'where did your side keep the facts about the "Rolling Stone" job?'

'In a file, of course,' said Leamas.

'What colour was it?' said Fiedler.

'Grey, with a red cross on it,' said Leamas.

'Did it have anything else on the outside?' Fiedler said.

'Yes, a list of names,' Leamas said. 'The names told

*See Chapter 16.

63

you who was allowed to use the file. It said that if anybody found the file he must give it back to one of the people named on the label.'

'Whose names were on the label?' Fiedler said.

'The Chief,' Leamas said, 'the Chief's secretary and Banking. That's all, I think. Oh yes! and Section 4.'

'Who else in Banking saw it?' Fiedler said.

'No one,' said Leamas. 'Only I did. No one else touched it.'

'Just you?' Fiedler said.

'Yes, just me,' Leamas said.

'Do you remember who brought it up?' Fiedler said. 'Did you ever go down to fetch it?'

Leamas shook his head.

Then suddenly he turned to Fiedler and said, 'Yes, yes I do! Of course I do. It was Peter. That's it. I once got it from Peter's room.'

'Peter Guillam?' said Fiedler.

'Yes,' said Leamas, 'Peter Guillam. Peter's name was on the label.'

'What part of the world did he deal with?' Fiedler said.

'East Germany,' Leamas said. 'He didn't have any spies working for him though. He was working on food supplies.'

'Did you talk to Peter about the file?' Fiedler said.

'No,' said Leamas. 'That's not allowed.'

'But,' Fiedler said, 'don't you think Peter may have had a spy, this "Rolling Stone", working for him?'

'No,' Leamas said. 'I told Peters. I was running things in Berlin. I would have known. "Rolling Stone" did not work in East Germany. How many times do I have to tell you?'

'Quite so,' said Fiedler softly. 'Of course you would have known.'

Fiedler went over to the window. He looked out. 'You should see it in the autumn,' he said. 'It's lovely when the beech trees are on the turn.'

21 Fiedler Follows Up 'Rolling Stone'

Fiedler loved to ask questions. Sometimes he just asked questions for the sake of it. They went out for a walk that afternoon. They went along the road down into the valley. All the time Fiedler asked questions. He asked about Leamas' headquarters, about the people who worked there. He asked about their pay, the holidays, the canteen. He asked about their love-life, their gossip. Most of all he asked what made them work there.

Leamas felt helpless. He did not know what Fiedler meant.

'Then tell me why you do it,' said Fiedler.

'Oh, for God's sake!' Leamas said.

They walked on in silence. But Fiedler was not put off.

'Why do you do it?' Fiedler said.

'I just think you Communists are bastards,' Leamas said.

Fiedler nodded.

'Yes,' he said. 'I understand that. It is stupid. But I understand it. What about the rest of your side? Do they all feel like that?'

'I don't know,' Leamas said. 'I've never talked to them about it. I suppose they don't like Communists.'

'Is that why your side is ready to lose so many spies?' Fiedler asked.

'I suppose so,' said Leamas. 'But I don't know. And I don't care.'

Fiedler smiled. 'I like the English,' he said quietly. 'My father liked them too. He was very fond of the English.'

'That gives me a nice, warm feeling,' Leamas said

sourly.

They stopped walking. Fiedler gave Leamas a cigarette and lit it for him.

*

'We'll sit down for a moment,' Fiedler said. 'Then we must go back. Tell me; this money you took to the foreign banks. What was it for?'

'What do you mean?' Leamas said. 'I've told you all about it. The money was for a spy.'

'A spy from behind the Iron Curtain?' Fiedler said.

'Yes,' Leamas said, 'I thought so.'

'Why did you think so?' said Fiedler.

'It was a hell of a lot of money,' Leamas said. 'Then the care I had to take. And, of course, my Chief was mixed up in it.'

'What do you think the spy did with the money?' Fiedler asked.

'Look!' Leamas said, 'I've told you. I don't know. I don't even know if he got it. I didn't know anything. I was just the office boy.'

'What did you do with the bank books?' Fiedler said.

'I took them back to London,' Leamas said, 'and I gave them in. And my false passport.'

'Did the foreign banks ever write to you?' Fiedler asked.

'I don't know,' Leamas said. 'I suppose any letters went to the Chief.'

'Did the Chief have a copy of your false signature?' Fiedler said.

'Yes,' Leamas said. 'I did lots of them. The Chief kept them.'

'More than one?' Fiedler said.

'Yes,' Leamas said. 'Whole pages of them.'

'I see,' said Fiedler. 'Then the Chief could have sent letters to the banks without your knowing?'

'Yes,' Leamas said. 'I signed a lot of blank sheets, too. But I don't *know* that any letters went. I didn't sit at my desk all day wondering about it. Anyhow I was hitting

66

the bottle a bit.'

'Yes,' Fiedler said. 'You said so. And, of course, I believe you.'

'I don't give a damn if you believe me or not,' Leamas said.

Fiedler smiled.

'I'm glad,' he said. 'You are a proud man, Leamas.'

Then Fiedler said, 'But you can help us find out if the spy did get this money. You could write to the banks and ask about the money. Ask for a bank statement. Do you think this would work? Will you do it?'

'It might work,' said Leamas. 'It depends if the Chief has written to the banks.'

'We have nothing to lose,' Fiedler said.

'But why do you want to know about the money?' Leamas said.

'If the money has been collected,' Fiedler said, 'we shall know where the spy was on a certain day. That could be very useful.'

'You'll never find him,' said Leamas. 'Once he's in the West, he'll disappear. What are you after? You don't even know if the man is an East German.'

Fiedler did not answer. He seemed to think this spy very important. He just looked across the valley.

Then he said, 'I can't tell you why I want to know about this one spy. But this "Rolling Stone" of yours was a job against us.'

'What do you mean "us"?' Leamas said.

'East Germany,' Fiedler said.

Leamas was watching Fiedler now.

'But what about me?' Leamas said. 'Suppose I don't write the letter to the banks? Isn't it time to talk about me?'

Fiedler nodded.

'Yes,' he said, 'Why not?'

'I've done my bit,' Leamas said. 'You and Peters have got all I know. I never agreed to write to banks. It could be dangerous to do that. That doesn't worry you, I know. I'm not important to you, am I?'

'Let me be frank,' Fiedler said. 'You've told us some things. But I must keep you with me. I might want to ask you some more questions. There is a lot you haven't said. In a month or two I may want to ask some more questions.'

'You mean you're going to keep me here?' Leamas said.

'Yes,' said Fiedler. 'A man who goes over to the other side has got to be patient. Not very many of them are patient enough.'

'How long do I have to stay?' Leamas said.

Fiedler was silent.

'Well?' Leamas said.

'I will let you go as soon as I can,' Fiedler said. He spoke very seriously. 'I can't lie to you. I could say one month, or less. But I don't know. And that is the truth. I've got to follow up some of the things you've said. When I've done this, you will need a friend. I will be that friend. You can trust me.'

They walked back to the house. There were no more questions.

As he lay in his room, Leamas thought about how things were going.

'Fiedler is on to it,' he thought. 'Just as the Chief said. We've laid our trap and Fiedler is walking into it. He's fallen for it. The Chief said that "Rolling Stone" would get Mundt. Perhaps Fiedler is going to do it for us.'

22 Leamas Writes a Letter

Leamas was still in bed the next morning when Fiedler came in. Fiedler brought him two letters to sign. Leamas read the first letter:

To the Manager,
The Royal Bank Ltd.,

Copenhagen

Dear Sir,

I have been away from England for some weeks, and so I have not had any letters. I wrote to you on March 3rd asking for a bank statement. I have not had a reply from you. Could you please send the statement to me at the following address:

13 Colombes Avenue,

Paris 12,

France.

I am sorry to give you this trouble.

Yours faithfully,

(Robert Lang)

'What is all this about a letter of March 3rd?' Leamas said. 'I haven't written a letter to them.'

'No,' said Fiedler, 'you haven't. As far as we know, no one has. That will worry the bank. If your Chief *has* written to them, they will think that the letter of March 3rd from you will have been about the same thing. They will send you a bank statement.'

The other letter which Fiedler brought was the same. Only the names were different. The address in Paris was the same.

Leamas took a blank piece of paper and his pen. He practised writing the name 'Robert Lang' a few times. Then he signed the first letter.

He then sloped his pen backwards and practised the second name, 'Stephen Bennett.' Then he wrote 'Stephen Bennett' at the end of the second letter.

'Very good,' said Fiedler. 'That's very good.'

'What do we do now?' Leamas asked.

'The letters will be posted in Switzerland tomorrow,' Fiedler said. 'Our people in Paris will phone the answers to me as soon as they come. We shall know in a week.'

'What shall we do until then?' Leamas said.

'We must stay together all the time,' Fiedler said. 'I

know you will not like that. I thought we could go for walks, drive round in the hills a bit. We must kill time. I want you to relax.'

Then Fiedler changed his tune.

'By the way,' he said, 'I could find you a girl friend, if you want one.'

'No, thank you,' said Leamas. 'I don't need someone to get me a girl. I'm not like you.'

'But you had a woman in England, didn't you?' Fiedler said, 'The girl in the library?'

Leamas turned on Fiedler, his hands open at his sides.

'One thing!' he shouted. 'Let me tell you just one thing! Don't ever talk about her again. Not as a joke, nor as a threat. If you do, I'll dry up. You will not get another bloody word out of me as long as I live. Tell that to them, Fiedler. Tell that to Mundt or whoever told you to say it. Tell them what I said.'

'I'll tell them,' Fiedler said. 'I'll tell them. But it may be too late.'

*

In the afternoon they went walking again. The sky was dark and heavy, and the air warm.

'I've only been to England once,' Fiedler said. 'I was on my way to Canada, before the war. I was a child then, of course. We were in England for two days.'

Leamas nodded.

'I can tell you this now,' Fiedler said. 'I nearly went to England a few years ago. I was going to take Mundt's place. Did you know that Mundt was once in London?'

'Yes,' said Leamas.

'I always wondered what Mundt's job would have been like,' Fiedler said.

'Usual sort of job, I expect,' Leamas said. 'You would have met a lot of people. You would have seen a bit of British trade.'

Leamas pretended to sound bored.

'But Mundt did a lot,' Fiedler said. 'He found it easy.'

'So I hear,' Leamas said. 'He even managed to kill a couple of people.'

'Ah yes,' Fiedler said. 'That was the Fennan case, wasn't it? I am surprised that Mundt escaped. It was surprising, wasn't it?'

'I suppose so,' said Leamas.

'How could the man escape?' Fiedler said. 'His photographs were everywhere. Everyone in Britain knew he was a wanted man.'

'I heard that the British didn't want to catch him,' Leamas said.

Fiedler stopped talking.

'What did you say?' he said.

'Well,' Leamas said, 'Peter Guillam told me that they didn't want to catch Mundt. Peter was sure that they did not really search for Mundt.'

'Are you sure of that?' Fiedler said. 'Are you sure that Guillam really said that? There was no search?'

'Of course I'm sure,' Leamas said.

'Did Guillam say anything else?' Fiedler said. 'Was there any other reason why they didn't want to catch Mundt?'

'What do you mean?' asked Leamas.

Fiedler shook his head. They walked on along the path. Leamas guessed that Fiedler was thinking hard.

'Mundt must have been mad,' Leamas said. 'You can't kill people in London and get away with it.'

'But Mundt did, didn't he?' Fiedler said. 'He did get away with it. And he did good work.'

*

'Tell me some more about Karl Riemeck,' Fiedler said. 'He met your Chief once, didn't he?'

'Yes,' said Leamas. 'In Berlin. About a year ago, perhaps a bit more.'

'Where did they meet?' Fiedler asked.

'In my flat,' Leamas said.

'Why?' Fiedler asked.

'The Chief always wanted to join in when things were going well,' Leamas said.

'Did you mind?' Fiedler said.

'No,' said Leamas. 'Why should I?'

'Karl was your spy,' Fiedler said.

'The Chief can meet anybody,' Leamas said. 'The Chief is different. And Karl enjoyed it.'

'Were the three of you together all the time?' Fiedler said.

'Not quite,' Leamas said. 'I left them for a quarter of an hour. The Chief wanted that. I left the flat. I pretended we had run out of whisky.'

'Do you know what they talked about when you were out?' said Fiedler.

'How could I?' said Leamas. 'Anyway, I wasn't interested.'

They walked on in silence for a while. Then Fiedler said, 'I'm beginning to like you, Leamas. But one thing puzzles me.'

'What is that?' Leamas said.

'Why you came here,' Fiedler said. 'Why ever you came over to us.'

Leamas started to say something, but Fiedler said, 'It wasn't very nice of me to say that, was it?'

23 More about Mundt

As each day passed Fiedler seemed to get more worried. Once they were out in the car. It was late in the evening. Fiedler stopped at a phone box. He left Leamas in the car and made a long phone call. When he came back to the car, Leamas said, 'Why didn't you phone from the house?'

Fiedler just shook his head.

'We must be careful,' he said. 'You must be careful, too.'

'Why?' said Leamas, 'What's going on?'

'Do you remember the money you paid into the Copenhagen bank?' said Fiedler. 'Do you remember the letter you wrote about it?'

'Of course,' said Leamas.

Fiedler did not say any more. They drove on into the hills. There they stopped. They were among tall pine trees.

'Whatever happens,' Fiedler said, 'don't worry. It will be all right. Do you understand?'

His slim hand was on Leamas' arm.

'You may have to look after yourself for a bit,' Fiedler said. 'But it won't last long. Do you understand?'

'No,' said Leamas. 'And since you won't tell me, I shall have to wait and see. But don't worry about me.'

'Do you know Mundt?' said Fiedler. 'Do you know about him?'

'We've talked about Mundt,' Leamas said.

'Yes,' Fiedler said, 'we've talked about him. He shoots first and asks questions afterwards. It's odd. Spies are supposed to ask questions. But Mundt doesn't.' Then, under his breath, Fiedler said, 'Perhaps he is afraid of the answers.'

.Leamas waited. After a moment Fiedler went on, 'He has never done a cross-examination before. He always leaves the questions for me. He always says, "You do the cross-examination. You ask the questions. I'll catch them. Then I'll hammer them."'

Fiedler went on, 'It used to be a joke between us. But when he began to kill, that was different. He killed one here, another there. Just as you said. He would not let me ask them any questions. He's a good spy, very good. But he's gone too far. Why does he do all this killing? Why, Leamas, why?'

Fiedler's hand was again on Leamas' arm, clasping

it tightly. The car was dark. Leamas knew that Fiedler was very tense.

'I've thought about it night and day,' Fiedler said. 'I've tried to find out why. I had to work it out. I couldn't help myself, Leamas. Mundt was afraid of something. He was afraid that we would catch a spy who would talk too much.'

'What are you saying?' Leamas said. 'You're out of your mind.'

Leamas sounded afraid.

'It all worked out, you see,' Fiedler said. 'Mundt got out of England so easily. You said so yourself. You said the British did not want to catch him. Why not? I'll tell you why. Mundt was their man. Mundt was a spy for the British. Don't you see? Mundt is working for you!'

'You are out of your mind,' Leamas said. 'Mundt will kill you if he thinks you say things like this. Shut up, Fiedler. And drive us home.'

At last Fiedler let go of Leamas' arm.

'You are wrong,' Fiedler said. 'We need each other. You have given me the answer I wanted.'

'It's not true,' Leamas shouted. 'I've told you again and again. My side could not have done it. I would have known. It just is not possible. You are trying to tell me that my Chief had the enemy leader on his side without me knowing! You are mad, Fiedler. You are damned well off your head.'

Leamas began to laugh.

'You want his job,' he said. 'You just want his job.'

For a moment there was silence.

Then Fiedler said: 'That money in Copenhagen. The bank has answered your letter. The money was called for one week after you paid it in. The bank told us the date. *On that date Mundt was in Copenhagen.*'

24 Invitation for Liz

Liz picked up the letter. It was from the Communist Party headquarters. She wondered what it was all about. She opened it. It was an invitation. It said:

'Dear Comrade,
We have just arranged for an English Communist visit to East Germany. Each person will be able to spend three weeks in East Berlin. This is a grand chance for our comrades to see the East Berlin Communists at work.

We asked your district to choose someone to go on this visit. Your district has chosen you. We want you to go if you possibly can. We know that the East German branch at Leipzig is ready to welcome you. We are sure that you are the best person for the job. We know that you will be a big success. We shall pay all your expenses.

We are sure that you will know that this is a big honour. The visit will take place at the end of next month, about the 23rd. Will you please tell us as soon as possible if you can go. Then we will send you all the details.'

Liz put the letter down. She could not understand how they even knew her name. No one at district headquarters knew her. She had met a few of the people who came to speak. Perhaps the last one had remembered. Liz tried to remember his name. For some time she couldn't. Then she remembered. It was Ashe. 'That's right,' she said to herself, 'Ashe. That was his name.' He had spoken to her for a long time. Perhaps he had given in her name. An odd man, he was. He had taken her out for coffee after the meeting.

He had asked her about her boy friends. He asked her lots of questions about herself, as well. He certainly knew a lot about East Germany.

Liz was sure it was Ashe. He must have told someone about her. And now she had got this invitation. It still seemed very funny. She read the letter again. It was on headquarters' writing paper. It had the usual thick red print at the top.

The more she read it, the odder it seemed. Such short notice. How could she get away from the library? Then she remembered. Ashe had asked her about her holidays. And it was such a long letter. Headquarters usually wrote very short letters.

Liz shrugged her shoulders. It was a chance to go abroad. And it was free. It sounded interesting. She had never been abroad. It would be fun. She didn't like Germans much. The Germans had killed her father. But she went to her desk and opened it. She took out a sheet of writing paper. She put the paper into her typewriter. She typed a neat letter saying that she would go.

As she closed her desk she saw the card Alec's friend George Smiley had left when he visited her. She remembered Smiley. She remembered him asking if Leamas knew she was a Communist.

'How silly to think of Alec all the time,' she thought.

Well, this trip would take her mind off him.

25 Arrest

Fiedler and Leamas drove back to the house from the wood. Fiedler did not say any more about Mundt. It was dusk. The hills were dark, like giant caves.

Fiedler parked the car in a shed at the side of the house. They got out and walked together to the front door. They were about to go into the house. They heard a shout. It came from the trees. Then someone called Fiedler's name. Leamas and Fiedler turned round. Leamas could just see three men standing. They were waiting for Fiedler to come.

'What do you want?' Fiedler said.

'We want to talk to you,' they said. 'We're from Berlin.'

Fiedler stopped. 'Where's that damned guard?' he said. 'There should be a guard on the front door.'

Leamas shrugged.

'Why aren't the lights on in the hall?' Fiedler said. Then he walked slowly back towards the three men.

Leamas waited for a moment. He could not hear anything. And so he went in through the dark house and into the small building behind it. This was where his bedroom was. It was a dirty hut, with pine trees all round it.

The hut was divided into three bedrooms. Leamas had the middle one. The room nearest the house was the bedroom of Leamas' guards. He had to go through this room to get to his. The far room was always locked. Leamas did not know who used that one. He knew it was a bedroom. He had looked in from outside. It had a single bed and a small desk. The bed was made and the desk had papers on it. He thought it must belong to another guard. This did not worry Leamas. He was used to being watched. He had always been watched when he worked in Berlin. He was good at his job. He always knew when people were following him and he could usually trick them. But this night he knew something was wrong. As soon as he went into the guard's bedroom he knew that things were not right.

The lights in the hut were put on and off from the house. It was only nine o'clock. The lights were already out. Usually they stayed on until eleven. But now they were out and the shutters were down.

He left the door open as he went into the guard's

bedroom. But the pale light from outside made little difference. He could only just see the two empty beds. He stood still and peered into the room. He was surprised that it was empty. Then the door behind him closed, perhaps by itself. Leamas did not try to open it. It was now pitch dark.

There was no sound. Leamas was on the alert. He smelt cigar smoke. It must have been in the air all the time. But he smelt it now for the first time. Like a blind man, the darkness made him smell things more keenly.

He had a box of matches in his pocket. But he did not use them. He took one step to the side, and pressed his back against the wall. Then he stood still. He knew that they were waiting for him to go into his own room. And so he stayed where he was. Then he heard a footstep. Someone was coming to the hut from the house. The door was rattled. Then he heard a key turn. He was locked in. Still he did not move. He was a prisoner.

Very slowly Leamas crouched. He put his hand in the side pocket of his coat. He was quite calm. But he remembered an army sergeant once saying to him, 'You've always got a weapon. An ash tray, a couple of coins, a pen. Anything will do. Never use both hands at once. Keep your left arm free and hold it across your belly. Keep your hands open and the thumbs stiff.'

Leamas took his box of matches in his right hand. He held it longways and crushed it. The small pieces of the box poked out between his fingers. Then he moved slowly along the wall until he came to a chair. He pushed the chair into the middle of the room. He did not care how much noise he made. He moved back from the chair and stood in the corner of the room.

As he did this he heard the door of his bedroom open. He tried to see who it was. But he could not, because there was no light in his room, either. It was completely dark. He dared not move forward to attack. The chair was in the middle of the room. This was a good thing for Leamas, because he knew it was there and they did not. But he had to make them attack him. He could not wait until the man who had locked the door had reached the house and put on the lights.

'Come on,' he said in German. 'I'm here, in the corner. Come and get me, can't you?'

Not a move, not a sound.

'I'm here,' he said again. 'Can't you see me? What's the matter, then? Come on, children, come on.'

Then he heard one coming. Then another followed. Then he heard one of them curse as he fell over the chair. That was what Leamas was waiting for. He threw his box of matches away and crept forward slowly. He came slowly on until his hand touched an arm. He felt the warm cloth of a soldier's uniform. Leamas tapped the soldier's arm twice. A frightened voice said quietly in German, 'Is that you, Hans?'

'Shut up, you fool,' Leamas said. Then, at the same time, he grasped the man's hair. He pulled his head forward and down. He drove the side of his right hand on to the man's neck. Then he pulled him up again by the arm and hit him in the throat with his open fist. Then he let him fall. As the man's body hit the ground, the lights went on.

In the doorway stood a young man. He was a captain of the People's Police. He was smoking a cigar. Behind him were two men. One was quite young. He held a pistol in his hand; Leamas thought it was a Czech pistol with a loading lever on the spine.

They all looked at the man on the floor. Somebody unlocked the outside door. Leamas turned to see who it was. There was a shout, telling him to stand still. Slowly he turned back and faced the three men.

He had his hands at his side when they hit him. The blow seemed to crush his skull. He fell, drifting warmly as he became unconscious.

*

79

When he woke up he heard singing, and a warder yelling, 'Shut up!'

Leamas opened his eyes. The pain burst on his brain like a bright light. He lay quite still, forcing his eyes to stay open. His feet were as cold as ice. He could smell the sour prison clothes.

He tried to lift his hand to touch the blood that was caked on his cheek. But his hands were behind him, locked together. His feet, too, were tied together. That was why they were cold. All the blood had left them.

Painfully he looked around, trying to lift his head an inch or two from the floor. He tried to stretch his legs, but his whole body was hit with a terrible pain. The pain was so terrible that he screamed aloud. This scream was like the last cry of a man being tortured on the rack.

He tried to straighten his legs again. At once the pain came back. But now he knew why. His hands and his feet were chained together behind his back.

They must have beaten him up while he was unconscious. His whole body was stiff and bruised. He wondered if he had killed the guard. He hoped so.

Above him shone a large, bright light. There was no furniture in the room. The walls were white. The room had a grey steel door. There was nothing else. Nothing at all. Nothing to think about. Just the savage pain.

He must have lain there for hours before they came. It was hot, because of the light. He was thirsty but he would not call out.

At last the door opened and Mundt stood there. He knew it was Mundt from the eyes. Smiley had told him about Mundt's eyes.

26 Mundt

They untied Leamas and let him try to stand. But his hands and feet had been tied for so long that he fell. They let him lie there and watched him on the ground. They were like children looking down at an insect.

One of the guards pushed past Mundt and shouted to Leamas to get up. Leamas crawled to the wall. He put his hands against the wall. He was halfway up when the guard kicked him and he fell again. Leamas tried again. This time the guard let him stand with his back against the wall. Then Leamas saw the guard move. He knew the guard was going to kick again, and so he threw himself at the guard and drove his head into the guard's face. They fell together. Leamas was on top. The guard got up. Leamas waited for him to get his own back.

Mundt spoke to the guard. Leamas was picked up by the shoulders and feet and carried down the corridor. He was terribly thirsty.

They took him to a small room. It was a comfortable room with a desk and armchairs. The furniture was good. Mundt sat at the desk and Leamas sat in an armchair. Leamas' eyes were half closed. The guards stood at the door.

'Give me a drink,' Leamas said to Mundt.

'Whisky?' Mundt said.

'No, water,' Leamas said.

Mundt filled a jug and put it on the table beside Leamas with a glass.

'Bring him something to eat,' Mundt said to one of the guards.

The guard left the room. He came back with a mug of soup and some sliced sausage.

Leamas ate and drank. They watched him in silence.

'Where's Fiedler?' Leamas said when he had finished eating.

'Under arrest,' Mundt said sharply.

'What for?' Leamas said.

'For trying to plot against the people,' Mundt said. Leamas nodded slowly.

'So you won,' he said. 'When did you arrest him?'

'Last night,' Mundt said.

Leamas waited for a moment. He was trying to look clearly at Mundt.

'What about me?' he said.

'You are an important witness,' Mundt said. 'Of course, you will stand trial later too.'

'So you will say that I was sent over from London to help frame Mundt, will you?' Leamas said.

Mundt nodded. He lit a cigarette and gave it to one of the guards to pass to Leamas.

'That's right,' he said.

The guard came over. He put the cigarette between Leamas' lips.

'You will also stand trial on another charge,' Mundt said quietly. 'Murder.'

'So the guard died, did he?' Leamas said.

As he said this a wave of pain went through Leamas' head.

'Yes,' Mundt said. 'The guard did die. So it will not matter much about your trial for being a spy. I have decided that Fiedler's trial will be in public.'

'And you want me to confess?' Leamas said.

'Yes,' Mundt said.

'In other words,' Leamas said, 'you haven't any proof against Fiedler.'

'We shall have proof,' Mundt said. 'We shall have your confession!'

Mundt did not use threats. He did not act. He just spoke coldly and quickly.

'But there is some hope for you,' Mundt said. 'You were blackmailed by your headquarters in Britain. They forced you into setting a trap against me. The court will be kind to you. We know that your Chief accused you of stealing money. There was nothing else you could do. You had to do what they wanted.'

'How did you know they accused me of stealing money?' Leamas said.

Mundt did not answer.

Then Mundt said, 'Fiedler has been very stupid. As soon as I read Peters' report about you, I knew why you had been sent. I knew it was a plot against me. I knew, too, that Fiedler would fall for it. Fiedler hates me so much. Of course your side knew that. It was a very clever plot. Who planned it? Tell me, was it Smiley? Did he do it?'

Leamas said nothing.

'I asked Fiedler to send me his report about you,' Mundt said. 'He kept putting it off. I knew then that I was right. Fiedler gave his report to the Council, my bosses, yesterday. But he did not send me a copy. Someone in London has been very clever.'

Leamas said nothing.

'You had lunch with Ashe, didn't you?' Mundt said. 'Ashe fell into your trap, didn't he?'

The banging in Leamas' head suddenly got worse. The room was dancing. He heard voices around him and the sound of footsteps. The room was full of people, all shouting. Then they were going, all marching away. There was silence. Then a cool cloth was put across his forehead and kind hands carried him away.

Leamas woke up on a hospital bed. At the foot of the bed stood Fiedler, smoking a cigarette.

27 Fiedler

Leamas looked around. He was lying on a bed, with sheets. He was in a hospital ward with no bars on the windows. The room had pale green walls. Fiedler was watching him, smoking.

A nurse brought Leamas some food: an egg, some thin soup and fruit. He felt like death. But he ate it. Fiedler watched.

'How do you feel?' Fiedler asked.

'Awful,' Leamas said.

'But better?' Fiedler said.

'I suppose so,' Leamas said. 'They beat me up.'

'You killed a guard,' Fiedler said.

'I guessed I did,' Leamas said. 'What did they expect me to do? What happened to you?'

'They softened me up, too,' Fiedler said.

'Mundt's men?' Leamas said.

'Mundt's men,' Fiedler said. 'And Mundt. Mundt had a special reason for beating me up.'

'Why?' Leamas said.

'Because I'm a Jew,' Fiedler said.

'Oh hell,' Leamas said softly.

'That is why I got special treatment,' Fiedler said. 'Mundt kept whispering to me. It was very strange.'

'What did he say?' Leamas said.

Fiedler did not answer. At last he said, 'It's all over now.'

'Why?' said Leamas. 'What has happened?'

'The day they got me I told the Council I wanted to prosecute Mundt as an enemy of the people,' Fiedler said.

'But you're mad,' Leamas said. 'You're raving mad, Fiedler, he'll never . . .'

'I had other evidence,' Fiedler said. 'As well as yours. I have been collecting evidence for the last three years. You gave us the final proof. That's all. I sent the Council a report about Mundt.'

'When did they get your report?' Leamas said.

'The day they caught us,' Fiedler said, 'I knew Mundt would fight. In the end he will lose. When we were in prison, they read my report. Now they know. They've arrested Mundt. He will appear in a secret court tomorrow.'

'What else have you found out about Mundt?' Leamas said.

'Wait and see,' Fiedler said. 'You will see tomorrow.'

'How does this court work?' Leamas said.

'There are three judges,' Fiedler said. 'They decide. Tomorrow I am going to speak against Mundt. Karden will defend him.'

'Who is Karden?' Leamas said.

'Karden is a very tough man,' Fiedler said. 'He looks like a country doctor. He is small and looks kind.'

'Why can't Mundt defend himself?' Leamas said.

'Mundt wanted Karden to defend him,' Fiedler said. 'They say that Karden has a witness.'

Leamas shrugged. 'That's your affair,' he said.

Leamas saw that Fiedler was excited and wanted to talk.

'What if Mundt is right?' Fiedler said. 'He asked me to confess, you know. Mundt said that I was to confess that I was working with British spies who were plotting to murder him. You see the case he can make out? That the whole thing was fixed by the British Intelligence to get me to bring the best Communist spy to his death.'

Leamas watched Fiedler carefully. He wondered if Fiedler had guessed.

Then Leamas said, 'Yes, Mundt tried that one on me, too. As if I had made up the whole story.'

'But what I mean is this,' Fiedler said. 'Would you

do this? Would you kill an innocent man?'

'Mundt's a killer,' Leamas said.

'But what if London wants to kill me?' said Fiedler. 'Would London do that?'

'It depends,' Leamas said. 'It depends on the need.'

'Ah,' Fiedler said. 'That is a great relief.'

'What do you mean?' Leamas said.

'You must get some sleep,' Fiedler said. 'Tomorrow you must talk.'

Soon Leamas was alseep. He was happy to think that Fiedler was on his side. Soon they would kill Mundt. Leamas had looked forward to that for a long time. His job was nearly done.

28 Liz in East Germany

Liz was happy in Leipzig. She was staying in a little house. The food was poor. But they talked about politics at every meal. Liz enjoyed speaking in German. She had learnt German from her aunt. In the evenings she went to political meetings.

At last, four days after she had come to Leipzig, their own Branch Meeting came. Liz had looked forward to this meeting for a long time. They expected a lot of people.

Seven people came.

Liz was terribly upset. She tried to pretend she didn't mind. But it was awful. It was worse than the meetings in London. It broke her heart.

At the end of the meeting Liz put on her coat. It was a cold evening. Liz was just going out through the door when a man appeared. He came out of the darkness. Just for a moment Liz thought it was Ashe. He was tall and fair. He wore one of those raincoats with leather buttons.

'I am looking for Comrade Gold,' he said. 'An

English Comrade.'

'I am Elizabeth Gold,' Liz said.

The man came into the hall. He closed the door behind him. The light shone full on his face.

'I am Holten,' he said. He showed some papers to the woman who had brought Liz to the meeting.

'I have a message for Comrade Gold,' Holten said. 'It is from the Council. The Council has asked you to come to a special meeting.'

'Oh,' said Liz. She did not know how the Council could have heard of her.

'The Council wants to show you their goodwill,' Holten said.

'But I ...' Liz began.

'I am sure your friend will not mind,' said Holten.

'Of course not,' said the woman.

'Where is this meeting?' Liz said.

'We must leave tonight,' Holten said. 'We must go a long way. Nearly to Gorlitz.'

'Gorlitz?' Liz said. 'Where is that?'

'East,' said Holten. 'On the border of Poland.'

'We can drive home now,' said Holten. 'You can collect your things. Then we must start at once.'

'Tonight?' said Liz. 'Now?'

'Yes,' said Holten.

A large black car was waiting for them. There was a driver in the front. The car had a flag on the bonnet.

It looked rather like an army car.

29 The Court

The court was about the same size as a classroom. At one end there were just five or six benches. Here sat guards among some spectators. Among the spectators were members of the Council.

At the other end of the room was an unpolished oak table and three tall chairs. The three judges of the court sat here. Above them, hanging from the ceiling, was a large red star made of plywood. The walls of the court were white. It was like Leamas' prison cell.

On each side of the table sat two men. They faced each other. One was middle-aged, about sixty, in a black suit and a grey tie. The other was Fiedler.

Leamas sat at the back. He had a guard on either side of him. Leamas could see Mundt among the spectators. There were policemen all round him. Mundt's fair hair was cut very short. He was wearing the usual grey prison uniform.

Leamas had not been long in his place when the President of the court rang the bell. Leamas looked up. He shuddered when he saw that the President was a woman. She was about fifty, with small eyes. Her hair was cut short like a man's. She wore a straight black tunic. She looked sharply round the room. She nodded to a guard to shut the door. Then she began to speak to the court:

'You all know why we are here,' she said. 'This is a secret court. Remember that. The Council has asked the court to meet.'

She pointed at Fiedler and said, 'Comrade Fiedler, you had better begin.'

Fiedler stood up. He nodded towards the judges. Then he took some papers out of his case.

He talked quietly and easily. Leamas thought he did it well.

*

'First of all,' Fiedler said, 'I must say this. On the day I sent in my report about Comrade Mundt, I was arrested. So was the traitor Leamas. Both of us were put in prison. Both of us were asked to say that we were plotting against Mundt because the British had asked us.

88

'You can see from my report how Leamas came over to us. We found him. We brought him over to Germany. Leamas did nothing to help us. He still thinks that Mundt is not a British agent. Leamas is *not* part of a British plot against us. He is not a "plant." We found Leamas. Leamas did not find us.

'I accuse Comrade Mundt of working for the British. He has given information to the British and he has taken money for it. The penalty for these crimes is death.'

Fiedler put his papers down.

'Comrade Mundt is forty-two years old,' Fiedler said. 'He is the head of the Department for the Protection of the People. He has always seemed a very clever man. He has always worked hard. But he became greedy. He could not resist the money which the British offered him.'

Fiedler paused. He looked round the room. Suddenly his eyes blazed. Leamas watched him.

'Let that be a lesson,' Fiedler shouted. 'Let that be a lesson to other enemies of the state.'

The spectators at the back of the court whispered to each other.

'Men like Mundt will not escape,' Fiedler said. 'The people will get them.'

Fiedler now opened the file that lay on the desk before him.

'At the end of 1956,' Fiedler said, 'Mundt was sent to London. He went as a spy. It was a very dangerous job and he did it well.

'At the end of Mundt's stay in London the British got him to join them. The British had found out that Mundt was a spy. They started a search for him. Ports were watched. His photograph was shown everywhere. But, after hiding for two days, Comrade Mundt went by taxi to London Airport and flew to Berlin. It was a bit *too* easy. I say that Mundt would not have escaped if the British had not helped him.'

The spectators at the back of the room whispered again.

'The truth is this,' Fiedler said. 'The British *did* catch Mundt. They told him to choose. Either he could go to prison for years. Or he could join the British side. The British said that they would pay him well, if he did. With the carrot in front of him and the stick behind him, Mundt joined the British side.

'Then the British made sure that Mundt got on well. I cannot prove that the British let Mundt murder their own spies. I cannot prove it. But I think it is very likely.

'Since 1960, when Mundt became head of his department, we have known that we had a spy amongst us. The British always seemed to have up-to-date information about us.

'Then, in 1961, I got a list of things which the British knew about us. It was a very full list. And it was right up to date. I showed it to Mundt, of course. He was my boss. He told me he was not surprised. He said he was dealing with it and I was to do no more. I thought then that perhaps Mundt had given the British the list. But it was too fantastic. And so I did not say anything.

'But, Comrades, the final proof has now come to us. I propose to call for this now.'

Fiedler turned round and looked towards the back of the room. 'Bring Leamas forward,' he said.

*

The guards on either side of Leamas stood up. Leamas came along the row to the gangway down the middle of the room. A guard told Leamas to stand facing the table. Fiedler stood just six feet away from him. First the President spoke to Leamas.

'Witness, what is your name?' she said.

'Alec Leamas,' said Leamas.

'What is your age?' she said.

'Fifty,' Leamas said.

'Are you married?' she said.

'No,' said Leamas.

'But you were,' she said.

'I am not married now,' Leamas said.

'What is your job?' she said.

'Librarian,' said Leamas.

Fiedler interrupted. He was angry.

'You used to be a British spy, did you not?' he said.

'Yes,' Leamas said. 'Till a year ago.'

'The judges have read your evidence,' Fiedler said. 'Please tell them now about what Peter Guillam told you in May last year.'

'You mean when we talked about Mundt?' Leamas said.

'Yes,' said Fiedler.

'I've told you,' Leamas said. 'I was at our headquarters in London. I met Peter Guillam in the corridor. We talked about Mundt. Peter Guillam said he thought the British did not want to catch Mundt.'

'If Mundt had been caught by your Secret Service,' Fiedler said, 'what would have happened to him?'

Leamas said, 'They would have asked him a lot of questions. Then they would have tried to exchange him for one of our men in prison over here. Or they would have got rid of him.'

'How?' said Fiedler.

'I don't know,' said Leamas. 'I've never been mixed up in that sort of thing.'

'Might they not have got him to act as a British spy?' said Fiedler.

'Yes,' said Leamas. 'But they didn't.'

'How do you know that?' said Fiedler.

'Oh, for God's sake, I've told you over and over again. If Mundt had been on our side I would have known. I couldn't help knowing.'

'Quite,' said Fiedler.

Fiedler seemed to be happy with that answer. Then he asked Leamas about the 'Rolling Stone' facts. He made Leamas tell the court about the money he had taken abroad. Fiedler said,

'Leamas took money to Copenhagen on June 15th. The money was taken from the bank there on June 21st. Mundt was in Copenhagen on June 21st. Then, on or about September 24th Leamas took money to Helsinki. On the third of October Comrade Mundt went on a secret visit to Helsinki.'

There was silence. Fiedler turned slowly and spoke again to the judges.

'Let me tell you something else,' he said. Fiedler turned to Leamas.

'Tell me, Leamas,' he said, 'what did Karl Riemeck do for you?'

'He was a spy for me,' Leamas said. 'He was shot by Mundt's men.'

'Yes,' Fiedler said. 'He was shot by Mundt's men. But before he was shot, he was a spy for the British.'

'Yes,' Leamas said. 'Karl Riemeck was one of the best spies we had. The Chief came to Berlin to meet him.'

'So the Chief trusted Karl?' Fiedler said.

'Oh yes,' Leamas said. 'Headquarters loved Karl.'

'Thank you,' said Fiedler. 'You may sit down.'

Leamas went back to his seat. Then Fiedler turned to the three judges.

'I want to talk to you about the spy Karl Riemeck,' Fiedler said. 'Riemeck gave the British a long list of facts about our side. He told them all our secrets. He told them all about the secret meetings of our Council. That was easy. He was the Secretary, and took the notes of each meeting.

'But he told the British other secrets. These secrets he could not have found out himself. Someone was telling Riemeck. And that someone was Mundt.'

Fiedler waited. Then he said quietly: 'The chain of command was Mundt-Riemeck-Leamas. Now Leamas says he does not know anything about Mundt. Leamas is a good spy. He will not talk about him. Leamas' masters in London have trained him well.'

The young man at the table lifted his pencil. He looked at Fiedler with his hard, cold eyes wide open. He said, 'Then why did Mundt have Riemeck shot if Riemeck was working for Mundt?'

'He had to,' Fiedler said. 'Our side suspected Riemeck. Riemeck's woman gave him away. Mundt told Riemeck to run. Then Mundt had him shot. Later, Mundt had the woman shot.'

Then Fiedler turned and looked straight at Mundt.

'There is your traitor,' Fiedler shouted. 'There is the man who has sold our secrets.

'I have nearly finished,' Fiedler went on. 'But I want to say one more thing. Mundt killed men to save himself. That is why, in the end, he had Karl Riemeck shot. That is why he had Riemeck's woman shot. No one could think of a worse crime than this.

'When you judge him, remember what a beast this man Mundt is. Death is too good for him.'

30 Leamas in the Witness Box

The President turned to the little man in the black suit.

'Comrade Karden,' she said, 'you are speaking for Comrade Mundt. Do you wish to ask Leamas any questions?'

'Yes, yes,' Karden said. 'I should like to in one moment.'

Karden got slowly to his feet. He put on his gold-rimmed glasses, pulling them over his ears. He looked a kind little man. His hair was white.

'Comrade Mundt says that Leamas is telling lies,' Karden said quietly. 'Mundt says that Comrade Fiedler has fallen into a plot or is part of it. Leamas and the British have plotted to catch Mundt. We agree that Karl Riemeck was a British spy. But Mundt was not part of it. Mundt did not take money to betray us.

There is no proof of this. We say that Leamas went back from Berlin to London and pretended to be a drunk. He got into debt and hit a shopkeeper so that our side would notice him. He pretended to be a traitor. We believe the British planned all this so that Leamas could come over here and plot against Mundt. Fiedler has fallen for this plot. Fiedler now wants to murder Mundt. Comrade Fiedler has made a big mistake. Or he has joined the British side to plot against us.

'Mundt has known for a long time what Leamas was doing. He read the reports of what Leamas said to Fiedler. Mundt has been asking questions, too.

'While Leamas was with Fiedler, Mundt sent men to London. These men asked a lot of questions about Alec Leamas. They found he had led a double life. They found that Leamas had made one mistake. It was a simple mistake.'

Karden paused. Then he smiled and said,

'We have a witness, too. You shall hear our witness, but not yet. Our witness is here. Comrade Mundt has had the witness brought here. A very clever move. Later I shall call that witness.'

Karden looked pleased. He seemed to be enjoying his little joke.

'But can I now ask Mr. Leamas one or two questions?' he said.

*

'Tell me,' Karden said to Leamas, 'do you have much money?'

'Don't be damned silly,' Leamas said. 'You know how I was picked up.'

'Yes indeed,' Karden said. 'That was very clever. Then you have no money?'

'That's right,' said Leamas.

'Have you friends who would lend you money?' Karden said.

'If I had,' Leamas said, 'I wouldn't be here now.'

'Thank you,' Karden said. 'Another question. Do you know George Smiley?'

'Of course I do,' Leamas said. 'He worked at Headquarters.'

'Has he left Headquarters?' Karden said.

'Yes,' said Leamas.

'Have you ever seen him since?' Karden said.

'Once or twice,' Leamas said.

'Have you seen him since you left Headquarters?' Karden said.

Leamas paused. 'No,' he said.

'He didn't visit you in prison?' Karden said.

'No,' Leamas said. 'No one did.'

'After you left prison,' Karden said, 'you were picked up, weren't you, by a man called Ashe?'

'Yes,' said Leamas.

'You had lunch with him in Soho,' Karden said. 'When you and Ashe parted, where did you go?'

'I don't remember,' Leamas said. 'Probably I went to a pub. No idea.'

'Let me help you,' said Karden. 'You went to Fleet Street in the end. Then you got on a bus. Then you went by bus, tube and car, to Chelsea. You didn't do it very well. Do you remember that? I can show you the report if you like. I have it here.'

'You're probably right,' Leamas said. 'So what?'

'George Smiley lives in Chelsea,' Karden said. 'That's my point. Your car took you to number nine Bywater Street. My spy told me that. Number nine is Smiley's house.'

'That's rubbish,' Leamas said. 'I should think I went to the Eight Bells. It's a pub I like.'

'You went by car?' Karden said.

'That's rubbish too,' said Leamas. 'I went by taxi, I expect. If I have money, I spend it.'

'But why did you do all that running?' said Karden.

'That's just rubbish,' Leamas said. 'Your spies were probably following the wrong man.'

'Let's go back to my question,' Karden said. 'You don't think George Smiley was interested in you after you left Headquarters?'

'No,' Leamas said.

'You don't think Smiley wanted to see you after you met Ashe?' Karden said.

'No,' Leamas said. 'I haven't any idea what you mean. But the answer is no. Smiley did not help me.'

Karden smiled. He seemed pleased with this answer.

Then he said, 'Oh yes. When you asked the grocer to let you have the groceries without paying, how much money did you have?'

'Nothing,' said Leamas. 'I had been broke for a week. Longer, I should think.'

'But,' said Karden, 'what had you lived on?'

'Bits and pieces,' said Leamas. 'I'd been ill. I had a fever. I had hardly eaten for a week. That made me nervous. I expect that is why I hit the grocer.'

'But the library still owed you money?' Karden said.

'How did you know that?' Leamas said sharply. 'Have you seen . . .'

'Why didn't you go to the library and get your money?' Karden said. 'Then you could have paid for your groceries.'

Leamas shrugged.

'I forgot,' he said. 'Probably because the library was closed on Saturday mornings.'

'I see,' Karden said. 'Are you sure that it is closed on Saturday mornings?'

'No,' said Leamas. 'It's just a guess.'

'Quite,' Karden said. 'Thank you. That's all I have to ask.'

Leamas was sitting down. The door opened. A woman came in. She was large and ugly. She wore a grey overall.

Behind her stood Liz.

31 Liz in the Witness Box

Liz came into the court slowly. She looked around her with her eyes wide open. She looked like a half-awake child coming into a brightly lit room. Leamas had forgotten how young she was. When she saw him sitting between two guards she stopped.

'Alec,' she said.

The guard beside her put his hand on her arm. He took her to the spot where Leamas had stood. It was very quiet in the court room.

'What is your name, child?' the President asked.

Liz said nothing. Her long hands hung at her sides. Her fingers were straight.

'What is your name?' the President said. She said it loudly this time.

'Elizabeth Gold,' said Liz.

'You are a member of the British Communist Party?' said the President.

'Yes,' said Liz.

Then Liz heard Leamas' voice. It was hoarse and ugly. It filled the room.

'You bastards!' Leamas shouted. 'Leave her alone!'

Liz turned in terror. She saw Leamas standing. His white face was bleeding. She saw a guard hit him with his fist; Leamas half fell. Then both guards jumped on him. They lifted him up and pulled his arms high behind his back. His head fell forward on his chest.

'If he moves again, take him out,' the President said.

Then she said to Leamas. 'You can speak again later if you like. Just wait.'

Then the President leaned forward and stared at Liz.

'Have you ever been told in the Communist Party how to keep a secret?' she said.

Liz nodded.

'And have you ever been told not to ask questions?' the President said.

Liz nodded again. 'Yes,' she said, 'of course.'

'Then you must remember that rule today,' the President said. 'We are going to ask you some questions. Your answers are very important. You must speak the truth. Then you will help the Communist Party.'

'But who is on trial?' Liz said. 'What has Alec done?'

The President looked at Mundt. 'Perhaps no one is on trial,' she said. 'It makes no difference.'

There was silence in the room. Then in a very quiet voice Liz asked, 'Is it Alec? Is it Alec who is on trial?'

'I tell you,' the President said, 'it is better for you not to know. You must tell the truth and go.'

Then the President said, 'Comrade Karden wants to ask you some questions. Not many. Then you shall go. Tell the truth.'

Karden stood up. He smiled in his kind way.

'Elizabeth,' he said, 'Alec Leamas was your lover, wasn't he?'

'Yes,' Liz said.

'Tell me,' Karden said. 'Was Alec a Communist?'

'No,' Liz said.

'Did he know you were a Communist?' Karden said.

'Yes,' Liz said, 'I told him.'

'What did he say when you told him, Elizabeth?' asked Karden.

Liz did not know what to say. The questions came so quickly. She did not have time to think. She did not know whether to lie. She knew that Alec was in danger.

'What did Leamas say?' Karden said.

'He laughed,' Liz said. 'He was above that kind of thing.'

'Tell me,' said Karden. 'Was he a happy man? Was he always laughing?'

'No,' Liz said, 'he didn't often laugh.'

'But he laughed when you told him you were in the Communist Party?' Karden said. 'Do you know why?'

'I don't think he liked Communists,' Liz said.

'Do you think he *hated* Communists?' Karden said.

'I don't know,' Liz said.

'Did Leamas hate things?' Karden said.

'No,' Liz said. 'No, he didn't.'

'But he hit a grocer,' Karden said. 'Now why did he do that?'

Liz didn't trust Karden any more. She didn't trust his soft voice and his good-fairy face.

'I don't know,' Liz said.

'But you thought about it?' Karden said.

'Yes,' said Liz.

'Well, what did you think?' Karden said.

'Nothing,' Liz said.

'Did you know Leamas was going to hit the grocer?' Karden said.

'No,' Liz said.

Karden smiled.

'When did you last see Leamas?' Karden said.

'I didn't see him after he went to prison,' Liz said.

'When did you see him last, then?' Karden said.

'The night before it happened,' she said. 'The night before he had the fight with the grocer.'

'The fight?' Karden said. 'It wasn't a fight, Elizabeth. The grocer never hit back, did he? He never had a chance. Not very sporting!

'Tell me,' he said, 'Where did you meet Leamas that night?'

'At his flat,' Liz said. 'He had been ill He had not been to work. He had been in bed. I had been coming to cook for him.'

'Did you buy his food as well?' Karden said. 'And do his shopping?'

'Yes,' Liz said.

'How kind,' Karden said. 'It must have cost you a lot of money. Could you afford it?'

'I didn't,' Liz said. 'I got the money from Alec. He . . .'

'Oh,' said Karden sharply. 'So Leamas *did* have some money?'

Oh God, Liz thought. Oh God, oh dear God, what have I said?

'He didn't have much money,' she said quickly. 'Not much. A pound or two pounds. Not more. He didn't have more than that. He couldn't pay his bills. He couldn't pay for the electric light or his rent. All his bills were paid afterwards by a friend. A friend had to pay, not Alec.'

'Of course,' Karden said quietly. 'A friend! A friend came and paid his bills. An old friend, perhaps. Did you ever meet this friend, Elizabeth?'

Liz shook her head.

'I see,' Karden said. 'What other bills did this friend pay? Do you know?'

'No,' Liz said. 'No.'

'Are you sure?' Karden said.

'I said I don't know,' Liz said.

'Did Leamas ever speak of this friend?' Karden said.

'No,' said Liz. 'I didn't think he had any friends.'

'Ah,' Karden said.

There was a terrible silence in the courtroom. Liz felt like a blind child. Everybody else understood Karden's questions. Only she didn't.

'How much money do you earn, Elizabeth?' said Karden.

'Six pounds a week,' Liz said.

'Have you any savings?' Karden said.

'A few pounds,' Liz said.

'How much is the rent of your flat?' Karden said.

'Two pounds fifty a week,' Liz said.

'That's quite a lot,' Karden said. 'Have you paid your rent recently?'

Liz shook her head. She was helpless.

'Why not?' Karden went on. 'Have you no money?'

Liz whispered, 'Someone has paid it all for me.'

'Who?' Karden said.

'I don't know,' Liz said. Tears were running down her face.

'I don't know,' she said. 'Please don't ask any more questions. I don't know who it was. Six weeks ago a bank sent me a thousand pounds. They said it was from a charity. You know everything. *You* tell me who sent it.'

Liz buried her face in her hands. She wept. No one in the court moved. At last she put her hands down from her face and stopped crying.

'Why didn't you ask someone about this money?' Karden said. 'Or do you often get presents of a thousand pounds?'

Liz said nothing.

'You didn't ask because you guessed,' Karden said. 'Isn't that right?'

Liz nodded.

'You guessed it came from Leamas or Leamas' friend, didn't you?'

'Yes,' Liz said. 'I heard that the grocer Alec hit got a lot of money after the trial. Lots of people were talking about it. I knew it must be from Alec's friend.'

'How very strange,' Karden said. 'How odd.'

Then he said, 'Tell me, Elizabeth, did anyone call to see you after Leamas went to prison?'

'No,' Liz said. That was a lie. But she knew now that they wanted to prove something against Alec. They wanted to know something about the money, or his friends or the grocer.

'Are you sure?' Karden said.

'Yes,' Liz said.

'But the woman next door says two men came to see you,' Karden said. 'Two men came soon after Leamas went to prison. Or were they just lovers, Elizabeth? Just lovers, like Leamas, who gave you money?'

'Alec *wasn't* just a lover,' Liz shouted.

'But he gave you money,' Karden said. 'Did the other men give you money too?'

'Oh God,' she said, 'don't ask . . .'

'Who were they?' Karden said.

Then Karden shouted: '*Who?*'

'I don't know,' Liz said. 'They came in a car. Friends of Alec.'

'*More* friends?' Karden said. 'What did they want?'

'I don't know,' Liz said. 'They told me to send for them if . . .'

'Send for them?' Karden said. 'Where from?'

'Chelsea,' Liz said. 'His name was Smiley. George Smiley. He told me to ring him up.'

'And did you?' Karden said.

'No!' said Liz.

Karden put down his papers. There was a deathly silence in the court. Karden pointed at Leamas and said in a quiet voice, 'Smiley wanted to know if Leamas had told her too much. Leamas had found a girl friend. That was the one thing Headquarters had not expected him to do. He had found a girl friend and he had wept on her shoulder.'

Then Karden laughed quietly, as if he could see a joke.

He said, 'Karl Riemeck did the same. He found a girl friend. Leamas has made the same mistake.'

32 More Questions for Liz

Karden picked up his papers. He began again:

'Did Leamas ever talk about himself?' he said.

'No,' said Liz.

'You don't know anything about his past?' Karden said.

'No,' Liz said. 'I knew he'd been in Berlin. He worked for the government.'

'Did he tell you he had been married?' Karden said.

There was a long silence. Then Liz nodded.

'Why didn't you see him after he went to prison?' Karden said.

'I didn't think he wanted me to,' Liz said.

'Did you write to him?' Karden said.

'No!' Liz said. 'Yes, once. I just told him I would wait for him.'

'When he came out of prison you didn't try to meet him?' Karden said.

'No,' Liz said.

'Did he have anywhere to go to?' Karden said. 'Did he have a job to go to? Did he have friends?'

'I don't know,' Liz said. 'I don't know.'

'In fact,' Karden said, 'you had finished with him, hadn't you? Did you find another lover?'

'No,' Liz said. 'I waited for him. I'll always wait for him.'

'Then why didn't you write to him?' Karden said. 'Why didn't you try to find out where he was?'

'He didn't want me to,' Liz said. 'He made me promise not to follow him.'

'So he expected to go to prison, did he?' Karden said.

Karden knew that he had won. He had proved that Leamas had plotted against Mundt.

'No,' Liz said. 'Leamas didn't know he was going to prison. No . . . I don't know. How can I tell you when I don't know?'

'And on that last evening,' Karden said, 'did Leamas make you promise again? Did he make you promise again not to follow him? Well, did he?'

'Yes,' said Liz.

'And you said goodbye?' Karden said.

'Yes,' said Liz.

'Was it late?' Karden said. 'Or did you spend the night with him?'

'After supper,' Liz said. 'Then I went home. Not straight home. I went for a walk first. I don't know where.'

'Did Leamas say why he was finishing with you?' Karden said.

'He didn't finish with me,' Liz said. 'He just said he had something to do. He had to get someone. One day he would come back. If I was still there and . . .'

'And you said you would always wait for him?' Karden said. 'You said you would always love him, I suppose!'

'Yes,' said Liz.

'Did he say he would send you money?' Karden said.

'He said I would be . . . looked after,' Liz said.

'Was that why you didn't ask questions when you got a thousand pounds?' Karden said.

'Yes,' Liz said. 'Yes, that's right. Now you know everything. You knew it all before. Why did you send for me if you knew it all?'

Liz was sobbing. Karden waited for her to stop sobbing. Then he said, 'You can see from this, Comrade President, that Leamas' Headquarters fixed it all. They made out that they had treated him badly so that he seemed to have a grudge against them. Leamas got sent to prison on purpose. When he came out, we had to think he would be glad of making some money and getting his own back on them. His girl friend and his bills were taken care of by his Headquarters. He gave us facts that were untrue. They were all aimed at getting rid of Mundt.

'That is all I want to say to defend Comrade Mundt.'

Then Karden looked at Leamas and at Fiedler.

'She is a fool,' he said. 'It is lucky, though, that Leamas met her. It has happened before. Once again we have found out about a plot against us because the plotters were weak.'

Karden bowed to the judges and sat down.

Leamas stood up. This time the guards let him alone. He was angry. He could not understand what Headquarters had done. He'd told Headquarters to leave Liz alone. But he saw now that they had gone to her as soon as he had left London. It was insane. They had paid all his bills. What were they trying to do? Leamas could not understand. This had not been part of the plot to get Mundt. What were they trying to do? Kill Fiedler? Were they trying to kill their own spy?

Leamas made up his mind. There was only one thing he could do. He had to save Fiedler and Liz. He had to save Fiedler. If he did, Liz would perhaps get away. Leamas thought that he had no hope himself.

How the hell did they know so much about him? He was quite certain that he had not been followed to Smiley's house that afternoon. How did they know he had stolen money at Headquarters? The Chief had planned that just for Headquarters to know. For God's sake, how?

Leamas was very ashamed. He walked slowly to the front of the court. He was like a man going to the hangman.

33 Leamas Confesses

'All right, Karden,' Leamas said.

Leamas' face was white and hard. It looked like a stone. He had his head back. He was very still. It was frightening.

'All right, Karden,' he said, 'let her go.'

Liz was staring at Leamas. Her dark eyes were filled with tears.

'No, Alec, no,' she said. 'Don't tell them. Whatever it is, don't tell them just because of me. I don't mind any more. I promise I don't.'

'Shut up, Liz,' Leamas said. 'It's too late now.'

Then Leamas looked at the President.

'She knows nothing,' he said. 'Send her home, I'll tell you the rest.'

The President paused.

Then she said, 'She can leave the court. But she must not go home until we have finished. Then we shall see.'

'She knows nothing, I tell you,' Leamas shouted. 'Karden is right. Don't you see? It was a plot. How could she know? She's just a girl from a stupid library. She's no good to you.'

'She is a witness,' said the President. 'Fiedler may want to ask her some questions.'

Fiedler seemed to wake up when the President said this. He looked at Liz for a moment with his deep brown eyes.

'She knows nothing,' he said. 'Leamas is right. Let her go.'

Fiedler's voice was tired.

'Do you know what you are saying?' the President said.

'Yes,' said Fiedler. 'She has said what she had to say. It was all very clever. Let her go. I have no questions for her.'

A guard unlocked the door. He called into the passage. A woman answered. Then they heard heavy footsteps. Fiedler stood up. He took Liz by the arm and led her to the door. As she got to the door she looked back at Leamas. But Leamas was staring away from her.

'Go back to England,' Fiedler said. 'You go back to England.'

Suddenly Liz began to sob. The woman put her arm round her shoulder and led her out. The guard closed the door. The sound of her crying faded away to nothing.

*

Leamas began to talk.

'There isn't much to say,' he said. 'Karden is right. It was a put-up job. It was a plot. When we lost Karl Riemeck, we lost our only good spy in East Germany.

All the others had gone. We could not understand why Mundt seemed to kill them as soon as they joined us.

'I came back to London then. I saw the Chief. Peter Guillam was there and George Smiley. The Chief had an idea. "Let's set a trap," he said. "Let's pretend Mundt is a spy on our side. How would we pay him?" We went on from there; we planned it backwards. We thought that your side would fall into the trap.

'My part in the plot was to pretend to go to pieces. I had to drink a lot. I had to get into money troubles. Everybody in Headquarters helped. They did it damned well. Then one Saturday morning I hit the grocer. You know all the rest. From then on your side fell for it. You dug your own graves.'

'Your grave, you mean,' Mundt said, quietly. 'And perhaps Fiedler's.'

'You can't blame Fiedler,' Leamas said. 'He just happened to be the man on the spot. He's not the only man on your side who would like to hang you, Mundt.'

'We shall hang *you*,' Mundt said. 'You killed a guard. And you tried to kill me.'

'Smiley always said the plot could go wrong,' said Leamas. 'Smiley's nerve has gone. He has not been the same since the Fennan case when you were in London, Mundt. But I can't understand why Headquarters paid all the bills. It must have been Smiley. He must have wrecked it all on purpose. It was mad. All that work! Why did he have to mess it up?'

Then Leamas turned to the judges.

'But you are wrong about Fiedler,' he said. 'He's not on our side. They used him, of course. They knew he hated Mundt. He's a Jew, isn't he? You all know what Mundt thinks about Jews? For God's sake, enough people have got mixed up in this. Don't kill Fiedler as well. Fiedler is all right, I tell you.'

Leamas looked at the judges. They were watching him. Not one of them moved. Their eyes were steady and cold.

Then Fiedler spoke.

'And you messed it all up, Leamas,' he said. 'Fancy an old dog like you messing it up. And all for a girl in a stupid library. Your Headquarters must have known. How odd!'

Fiedler turned to Mundt.

'They knew that you would check everything, Mundt,' he said. 'Then why did they make all those mistakes? Why did they send money to the grocer? Why did they pay the rent? Why did they pay a thousand pounds to a girl in the Communist Party? What a risk!'

Leamas shrugged.

'We couldn't stop the plot once we had started it,' he said. 'We never expected you to bring me here. And I never thought you would bring the girl. I've been a damned fool.'

'But Mundt hasn't,' Fiedler said. 'Mundt knew what to look for. He knew the girl would give him the proof he wanted. Very clever of Mundt! He even knew about the thousand pounds. How did he find that out?'

There was silence. Then the President said, 'I think that the judges can now decide. Do you want to say any more, Fiedler?'

Fiedler shook his head. He was smiling about something.

'Then Fiedler must give up his position as Mundt's deputy,' the President said. 'All the judges agree. Later the Council will decide what to do with him. Comrade Mundt will decide what to do with the spy Leamas.'

The President looked at Mundt. But Mundt was looking at Fiedler. Mundt looked like a hangman trying to decide which rope to use to hang Fiedler.

And then, suddenly, Leamas understood what he had been sent to do. He had been sent to get *Fiedler*, not Mundt. It was Fiedler the Chief wanted out of the way, not Mundt. Mundt *was* a British spy. Fiedler had found out. And so Leamas had been sent to bring Fiedler to his death.

Leamas suddenly knew that a dreadful trick had been played.

34 Liz in prison

Liz stood at the window. She was staring into the tiny yard outside. She felt sick and terribly tired. Her legs ached. Her face felt stiff from weeping. She was dirty. She longed for a bath.

'Why don't you eat,' the woman guard said. 'It is all over now.'

'I'm not hungry,' Liz said.

The woman shrugged. 'You may have a long journey. There may not be much to eat at the other end.'

'What do you mean?' Liz said.

'The workers are starving in England,' the woman said. 'The bosses let them starve.'

Liz said nothing. There seemed no point in saying anything.

'What is this place?' she said.

'Don't you know?' said the woman. 'Ask them over there.'

The woman pointed at the window.

'Who are they?' Liz said.

'Prisoners,' the woman said.

'What kind of prisoners?' Liz said.

'Spies,' the woman said. 'Enemies of the state.'

'How do you know they are spies?' Liz said.

'The Party knows,' the woman said. 'The Party knows everything. Don't you know that?'

'But what have they done?' Liz said.

'They think that people are more important than the state,' the woman said. 'Communism cannot be made strong unless we all give up our rights as single people.' She went on to tell Liz about her work in the prison. Then Liz asked her:

'What will happen after the trial?'

'They will shoot Leamas,' the woman said. 'And the Jew, Fiedler.'

'What has Leamas done?' Liz said.

'He killed a guard,' the woman said.

'Why?' Liz said.

The woman shrugged.

'Will they shoot Fiedler too?' Liz said.

'Yes,' the woman said. 'He plotted against Comrade Mundt. Jews are all the same. Comrade Mundt knows what to do with Jews. We don't want them here. They say that Leamas and Fiedler plotted against Mundt.' The woman looked at the food in front of Liz, and went on, 'Are you going to eat that?'

Liz shook her head.

Liz went back to the window. She thought about Leamas. He had not looked at her when they took her out of the court room. She had failed him. She had destroyed two human beings, Leamas and Fiedler. Why did it have to be Fiedler? He had been kind to her. Why not the man with the short blond hair who had been smiling all the time as if it were all a big joke.

'Why are we waiting here?' Liz said to the woman.

'We must stay until they decide what to do with you,' the woman said.

'But what has Leamas done?' Liz said.

'He plotted against us,' said the woman.

'How could he?' Liz said. 'He was in England.'

'Perhaps Fiedler brought him over,' the woman said. 'But it is secret.'

The telephone rang. The woman picked it up. After a moment she looked at Liz.

'Yes, Comrade,' she said into the phone. 'At once.' Then she put the telephone down.

'You must stay,' she said. 'Comrade Mundt wishes it.'

'Who is Mundt?' Liz said.

'The Council wishes it,' the woman said.

'I don't want to stay,' Liz said. 'I want . . .'

'You must stay,' the woman said. 'The Party wishes it.'

'Who is Mundt?' Liz said again.

But the woman did not answer.

The woman took her out of the room. Liz followed her along endless corridors. They went past guards, down stairs, across yards. They were under the ground. Liz thought she was going right down into hell.

And no one would even tell her if Leamas was dead.

35 Liz has a Visitor

Liz heard a footstep outside her cell. There was some-one in the corridor. She did not know what time it was. It could have been five o'clock in the evening, or mid-night. She was in the dark. The silence was terrible. She longed for a sound. She had cried out once. But there had been no answer. There was not even an echo.

Suddenly the door of her cell opened.

A man came in. Liz knew who it was at once. The light behind him shone on his short fair hair.

'I am Mundt,' he said. 'Come with me, at once.' His voice was quiet.

Liz was terrified. She stood by the bed. She did not know what to do.

'Hurry, you fool,' Mundt said.

He took hold of her wrist. He pulled her out into the corridor. She watched him lock the door behind them. He took her arm roughly and pushed her along the corridor, half running, half walking. When they came to the end of a corridor Mundt would stop. Then he would go ahead and see if anyone was coming. Then he would signal to her.

Suddenly Mundt stopped. He thrust a key into a metal door. Liz waited. She was terrified. He pushed the door open. The sweet, cold air blew against her face. He signalled to her again. She followed him down two steps on to a gravel path. The path led through a rough kitchen garden.

They went along the path to a large gateway. They went through the gateway on to the road. A car was parked near the gateway. Standing by the car was Alec Leamas.

*

Liz started to move forward.

'Keep your distance,' Mundt said. 'Wait here.'

Mundt went forward on his own. For a long time the men talked together. Liz's heart was beating fast. She was shivering with cold and fear. At last Mundt came back.

'Come with me,' he said.

He took her to Leamas. Mundt and Leamas looked at each other for a moment.

Then Mundt said,

'Goodbye, Leamas. You're a fool. She's trash, like Fiedler.'

Then Mundt turned round. He walked off into the dark.

Liz put out her hand and touched Leamas. He turned away and opened the car door.

'Get in,' he said.

'Alec,' she said, 'what are you doing? Why is Mundt letting you go?'

'Shut up,' Leamas said. 'Don't think about it. Just get in.'

'What did he say about Fiedler?' Liz said. 'Why is he letting us go?'

'Because we have done our job,' Leamas said. 'Get in the car, quick!'

Liz got in and shut the door.

'What have you agreed with Mundt?' she asked.
'They said in the trial that you had plotted against him.
Then why is he letting you go?'

Liz's voice sounded afraid.

Leamas had started the car. He was soon driving fast
along the narrow road. On either side were bare fields.
In the distance there were dark hills. Leamas looked at
his watch.

'Were you worried about me?' Liz said. 'Is that why
you made Mundt let you go?'

Leamas said nothing.

'You and Mundt are enemies, aren't you?' Liz said.

Leamas still said nothing. He was driving fast now.
The road was bumpy. He had his headlights full on.
He did not dip them for other drivers. He drove
roughly, leaning forward. His elbows were almost on
the wheel.

'What will happen to Fiedler?' Liz said.

This time Leamas answered her.

'He will be shot,' he said.

'Then why didn't they shoot you?' Liz said. 'You
plotted with Fiedler against Mundt. You killed a
guard. They said so. Then why has Mundt let you go?'

'All right,' Leamas shouted. 'I'll tell you. I'll tell you
something you were never supposed to know. Something *I* was never supposed to know. Mundt *is* a British
spy. He works for our Headquarters. I guessed this at
the end of the trial. Only Headquarters could have
told Mundt about the money I was supposed to have
stolen. About my visit to Smiley's house. About the
money you got. And all the other things.

'Headquarters sent us here to save Mundt. Fiedler
had found out about Mundt. Headquarters have sent
us to save Mundt and kill Fiedler. Now you know. And
God help us both.'

36 The Wall

'If that is true,' Liz said, 'how do I fit into Headquarters' plot?'

'I don't know exactly,' Leamas said. 'I can only guess. Mundt told me a bit about it. He told me that Fiedler had found out about him. Mundt could not get rid of Fiedler. So Headquarters did it for him. They had to show the Communists that Mundt was not a British spy. Headquarters told me to frame Mundt. They said he had to be killed. I agreed. It was going to be my last job. So I acted like a drunk and punched the grocer. You know all about that.'

'And made love?' Liz said.

'No,' Leamas said. 'They didn't tell me to fall in love with you.'

Then Leamas said,

'But the point is this. Mundt knew all about it. He knew the plan. Mundt and Fiedler picked me up. Then Mundt let Fiedler take over. Mundt knew that Fiedler would fall for it. Fiedler thought Mundt was a British spy. Then I told him the same thing.'

Leamas paused. Then he said, 'Your job, Liz, was to make my story seem wrong. Then Mundt would be saved.'

'But how did Headquarters know about me?' Liz said. 'How did they know that we would meet? How did they know that we would fall in love?'

'They didn't,' Leamas said. 'They chose you because you were young and pretty. And because you were in the Communist Party. They knew you worked in that library. They sent me there on purpose. All we had to do was meet. Then, afterwards, they would send you money and make it look like an affair. We just made it easy for them.'

'Yes, we did,' Liz said. 'Oh Alec, I feel dirty.'

Leamas said nothing.

'Mundt wanted to keep me in prison, didn't he?' Liz said. 'I know too much, don't I?'

'Oh! for God's sake,' Leamas said.

'But why did Mundt let me go?' Liz said. 'I'm a risk to him, aren't I?'

'I expect he wants to blame someone for your escape,' Leamas said. 'He can kill some more people, then.'

'Innocent people?' Liz said. 'It does not seem to worry you much.'

'Of course it worries me,' Leamas said. 'But it is all part of my job. People who play this game take risks. Fiedler lost and Mundt and London won. It was a foul plot. But it has worked. That's all that matters.' Leamas nearly shouted the last words.

'They have done a wicked thing, Alec,' Liz said. 'How can you kill Fiedler? He was good, Alec. I know he was. And Mundt . . .'

'What the hell are you complaining about?' Leamas said. 'You are a Communist. Your Party is always at war, isn't it? One man is not important. It is the Party that matters. Isn't that what it says? At least you are still alive. At least Mundt has let you go.'

'But they let me love you,' Liz said. 'And you let me trust you.'

'They used us,' Leamas said. 'They cheated us both. They had to. It was the only way. Fiedler had nearly won. Mundt was nearly caught. Can't you understand?'

'But Fiedler was kind and good,' Liz said. 'He was only doing his job. Now you have killed him. Mundt is a spy and a traitor. But you help him. Mundt is a Nazi. He hates Jews. What side are you on?'

'There is only one rule in this game,' Leamas said. 'Mundt is on Headquarters' side. He gives them what they want. They need him. I hated Mundt. But I work for them. And so I've saved him.'

'But what about Fiedler?' Liz said. 'Don't you feel anything for him?'

'This is war,' Leamas said. 'It's nasty because you know the people. But it is only a small war. It's not as bad as the other wars. It's not as bad as the last war – or the next.'

'Oh God,' Liz said. 'You don't understand. What they have made us do is worse than war. They have used ordinary people like you and me to kill Fiedler.'

Leamas shouted at her, 'But what else have men done since the world began? I'm sick of killing. But I don't see what else they can do. They are only trying to stop people blowing each other up.'

'You're wrong,' Liz said. 'They are worse than all of us.'

Then Liz said, 'And it makes you the same, Alec. It makes you the same as Mundt. I should know. I am the one who has been kicked about. I've been kicked about by them, and by you, because you don't care. Only Fiedler cared. But the rest of you – you all treated me as if I was nothing. You're all the same, Alec.'

'Oh Liz,' Leamas said, 'for God's sake believe me. I hate it. I hate it all. I'm tired. But it is the world. It's men who have gone mad. Everywhere is the same. People are cheated. People are shot or put in prison. Your Party does it. God knows. Your Party was built on the death of ordinary people. You've never seen men die as I have.'

As Leamas spoke, Liz remembered the prison she had been in.

Suddenly Leamas went stiff. He peered through the car's windscreen. In the headlights of the car Liz saw a man standing in the road. He held a tiny light. He turned it off and on as the car got nearer.

'That's him,' Leamas said.

Leamas switched off the lights and the engine. They

glided silently to the man.

Leamas opened the rear door.

Liz did not turn round as the man got in. She just stared stiffly on into the rain.

*

'Drive at thirty miles per hour,' the man said. His voice was frightened. 'I'll tell you the way. When we reach the place you must get out and run to the wall. The searchlight will shine at the point where you must climb the wall. Stand in the beam of the searchlight. When the light moves away, begin to climb. You will have ninety seconds to get over. You go first,' he said to Leamas. 'The girl will follow you. There are iron rungs in the lower part of the wall. After that you must pull yourself up as best you can. You will have to sit on top and pull the girl up. Do you understand?'

'We understand,' Leamas said. 'How long have we got?'

'If you drive at thirty miles per hour we shall be there in about nine minutes,' the man said. 'The searchlight will be on the wall at five past one exactly. They can give you ninety seconds. Not more.'

'What happens after ninety seconds?' Leamas said.

'They can only give you ninety seconds,' the man said again. 'Otherwise it is too dangerous. Only one group of guards knows about it. They think you are Communist spies going into West Berlin. They have been told not to make it too easy for you. Ninety seconds are enough.'

'I bloody well hope so,' Leamas said. 'What time do you make it?'

'I checked my watch with the sergeant in charge of the guards,' the man said. 'It is twelve forty-eight. We must leave at five to one. Seven minutes to wait.'

They sat in total silence, except for the rain pattering on the roof. There was no one about. Above them the sky was lit with searchlights. Far to the left Leamas saw a flickering light, high up.

'What is that?' he said.

'Those lights flash the news into East Berlin,' the man said. 'The lights are high up on a scaffolding.'

'Of course,' Leamas said.

Leamas knew that they were very near the end of the road.

'You cannot turn back now,' the man said. 'Mundt told you that. You haven't got another chance.'

'I know,' Leamas said.

'If something goes wrong,' the man said, '– if you fall or get hurt – don't turn back. The guards shoot on sight at anyone near the wall. You *must* get over.'

'We know,' Leamas said. 'Mundt told me.'

'As soon as you get out of the car,' the man said, 'you are near the wall.'

'We know,' Leamas said. 'Now shut up.'

Then Leamas said

'Are you taking the car back?'

'Yes,' the man said. 'As soon as you get out I shall drive the car away. It is dangerous for me, too.'

'Too bad,' Leamas said.

Again there was silence. Then Leamas said,

'Have you got a gun?'

'Yes,' said the man, 'but I can't give it to you. Mundt said I mustn't. He said you would ask for it.'

Leamas laughed quietly.

'He would say that,' he said.

Leamas pulled the car's starter. The noise seemed to fill the street. The car moved forward slowly.

They went forward for about three hundred yards. Then the man said, 'Go right here, then left.'

They swung into a narrow side street. There were empty market stalls on both sides. The car only just passed between them.

'Left here, now!' the man said.

They turned again. Leamas was driving fast now.

They were among tall buildings. It looked like a dead-end. There was washing across the street. As they got near the dead-end the man said:

'Left again. Follow the path.'

Leamas went up onto the pavement. He drove along a wide footpath. It had a broken fence to the left and a building with no windows on the right. They heard a shout from above them. It was a woman's voice. 'Oh shut up,' Leamas said. He drove round a right-angle bend. He came to a main road.

'Which way?' he said.

'Straight across,' said the man. 'Go past the Chemist. Over there!' The man was leaning forward now. His face was close to Leamas' and Liz's. He pointed with his finger pressed against the windscreen.

'Get back,' Leamas said. 'Get your hand away. How the hell can I see if you wave your hand around like that?' Then Leamas asked,

'Where are we going?'

'We're nearly there,' the man said. 'Go slowly now. Left! Go left!' They drove under a narrow arch into a yard. Half the windows of the buildings were missing or boarded up. At the other end of the yard was an open gateway.

'Through there,' the man said. 'Then turn hard right. You will see a street lamp on your right. The next one is broken. When you reach that one switch off your engine. Then go on until you see a post box. That's the place.'

'Why the hell didn't you drive?' Leamas said.

'Mundt said you must drive,' the man said. 'Mundt said it was safer.'

They drove through the gate and turned right. They were in a narrow street, pitch dark.

'Lights out!' the man said.

Leamas switched off the lights and drove slowly forwards to the first street lamp. They could just see the second lamp ahead. It was broken. Leamas switched off the engine and the car went silently past it. Twenty yards ahead they saw the post box. Leamas put on the brakes. The car slowly stopped.

'Where are we?' Leamas whispered

'Pankow,' said the man. 'Near Pankow.'

Then the man pointed down a side street to the left. 'Look,' he said.

At the end of the street they saw the wall. It looked grey-brown. A searchlight shone on it. Along the top they saw three rows of barbed wire.

'How will the girl get over the barbed wire?' Leamas said.

'It has been cut where you climb,' the man said. 'There is a small gap. You have one minute to reach the wall. Goodbye.'

They got out of the car. Leamas took Liz by the arm. She jumped away from him as if he had hurt her.

'Goodbye,' said the German.

Leamas just said, 'Don't start that car until we are over.'

Liz looked at the German for a moment in the pale light. She saw his young, frightened face. He was only a boy trying to be brave.

'Goodbye,' said Liz.

Then she took her arm away from Leamas' and followed him across the road. They went into the narrow street that led towards the wall.

As they went into the street they heard the car start behind them. It turned and went back the way they had come.

'That's right,' Leamas muttered. 'You're all right, you bastard. Don't worry about us!'

Liz hardly heard what Leamas said.

37 In from the Cold

Leamas and Liz walked quickly. Leamas kept looking back over his shoulder to see if Liz was following. They reached the end of the street. Leamas stopped. He went into a doorway and looked at his watch.

'Two minutes,' he whispered.

Liz said nothing. She just looked at the wall and the ruined buildings behind it.

'Two minutes,' Leamas said again.

They had to cross a strip of thirty yards. About seventy yards away, to the right, was a watch tower. It had a searchlight. The light was shining on the strip of ground in front of the wall. Rain had begun to fall. There was no one about. Not a sound. It was like an empty stage. The lights were pale in the rain.

The searchlight moved slowly along the wall towards them. Each time it stopped they saw the bricks of the wall. As they watched the light stopped in front of them.

Leamas looked at his watch.

'Ready?' he said.

Liz nodded.

Leamas took her arm. They walked slowly across the strip of land. Liz wanted to run. Leamas held her so tightly that she could not. They were halfway towards the wall now. Leamas kept Liz very close to him. He was afraid that Mundt would not keep his word, and would take Liz away at the last moment.

They were almost at the wall. The light moved away to the north. They were left in total darkness. Leamas still held Liz's arm. He led her forward in the darkness. He had his other hand out in front of him to feel the wall. Suddenly he felt the rough brick. Now he could just see the wall. He could see the three lines of barbed wire and the cruel hooks holding it. There were metal rungs in the wall. Leamas took hold of the highest one. He pulled himself quickly up. He reached the top of the wall. He tugged at the lower line of the barbed wire. It came towards him. It had been already cut.

'Come on,' he whispered. 'Start climbing.'

He lay flat on the top of the wall and reached down. Liz stretched up her hand. Leamas took hold of it. He began to drag her slowly up. Her foot reached the first metal rung.

Suddenly everything burst into flame. From everywhere huge lights came on. All the lights blazed on Leamas and Liz.

Leamas was blinded. He turned his head away and pulled hard on Liz's arm. Now she was swinging free. He thought she had slipped. He shouted to her, still dragging her upwards. He could not see anything. He was still blinded by lights.

Then the sirens started to wail. Men started to shout orders. Leamas got to his knees. He took both Liz's arms in his. He dragged her up inch by inch. He was nearly falling.

Then they fired.

They fired three or four shots. Leamas felt Liz shudder. Her thin arms slipped from his hands. He heard someone shouting from the Western side of the wall.

'Jump, Alec! Jump, man!'

Now everyone was shouting, in English, French and German.

Leamas heard the voice of George Smiley. Smiley said,

'The girl, where's the girl?'

Leamas put up his hands to shade his eyes. He looked down at the foot of the wall. He could just see her. She was lying still.

For a moment he waited. Then, quite slowly, he

climbed back down the same rungs. He stood beside her. She was dead. Her face was turned away. Her black hair lay across her cheek as if to protect her from the rain.

They seemed to wait before firing again. Then someone shouted an order. Still no one fired.

At last they shot Leamas. Two or three shots. He stood, glaring all round like a blinded bull in an arena.

As he fell Leamas saw in his mind a small car. In it were some children. The small car was smashed between great lorries. The children were waving cheerfully through the car window as the lorries hit it.